Internal Control in Canadian Corporations:
a management perspective

Internal Control In Canadian Corporations
a management perspective

by Lois D. Etherington, PhD and Irene M. Gordon, PhD

The Canadian Institute of
Chartered Accountants

The Society of Management
Accountants of Canada

This Study expresses the views of the authors and has not been adopted, endorsed, approved, disapproved or otherwise acted upon by a Committee, the governing body or membership of the CICA or SMAC.

This Study is intended to stimulate thought, discussion and debate on matters of accounting and auditing theory and practice. Comments from readers on the matters dealt with in the Study would be welcomed.

ISBN 0-88800-126-6

TABLE OF CONTENTS

FOREWORD

In 1980, the CICA/SMAC Joint Committee on Co-operation agreed that each body should explore joint ventures in research. After consideration of a number of topics by the CICA Accounting Research and Auditing Standards Committees and the SMAC Accounting Principles and Practices Committee, the topic of Internal Control in Canadian Corporations was selected. The selection of the topic followed consideration of a project proposal submitted by Dr. Lois D. Etherington and Dr. Irene M. Gordon of Simon Fraser University, Burnaby, and it was agreed that the project should be undertaken on a joint author basis with the assistance of an advisory group, with representation from both CICA and SMAC. The project began in 1983.

This study is a fact-gathering and analytical exercise to gain a better understanding of Canadian business practices for establishing, monitoring and evaluating internal control systems. More specifically, the terms of reference for the study were to:

1. Ascertain what management perceives to be the objectives of internal controls.

2. Compare management's perceptions with the *Handbook* material on management's objectives for internal controls (see *CICA Handbook*, Section 5205).

3. Examine management's understanding of what constitutes internal control. Issues addressed would include:
   • Management's definition of internal control.
   • Establishment of guidelines for internal control systems related to the degree of risk.
   • The distinction made between preventive and detective controls.
   • The emphasis given to establishing controls in computerized systems.
   • The degree to which internal control is considered necessary.

4. Ascertain management's perception of who is responsible for the system of internal controls (who approves and designs the system, maintains it, evaluates its effectiveness and authorizes changes.)

5. Ascertain the lines of responsibility for reporting the effectiveness of internal control systems to:
   • Financial management.
   • Senior management.
   • Board of directors or audit committees.

6. Identify and investigate specific internal control problems from the viewpoint of:
   • Chief financial officers.
   • Systems managers.
   • Internal auditors.

7. Identify and investigate potential risks associated with inadequate internal controls.

The study is specifically directed to management (including chief financial officers, systems managers and internal auditors), members of audit committees and external auditors, although it will also be of interest to other audiences.

The Research Departments of the CICA and SMAC appreciate the enthusiasm and interest that the authors have committed to this project and acknowledge the depth and quality of the research. The time and effort devoted by members of the advisory group to this project is also most appreciated. Thanks are also expressed to those company officials who responded to questionnaires or provided interviews with the authors. The assistance provided by A.R. Salole, CICA Senior Research Studies Manager, is also acknowledged.

D.P. Armishaw, RIA
Director of Research
The Society of Management
Accountants of Canada

D.J. Moore, CA
Research Studies Director
The Canadian Institute of
Chartered Accounts

April, 1985

Authors

L.D. Etherington, Ph.D.
Simon Fraser University
Burnaby

I.M. Gordon, Ph.D.
Simon Fraser University
Burnaby

Advisory Group

J.D. Blazouske, MBA, FCA, RIA, FSMAC
Concordia University, Montreal
M. Gibbins, Ph.D., CA
University of Alberta, Edmonton
(formerly University of British Columbia, Vancouver)
J.G. Podmore, RIA
West Coast Transmission Ltd., Vancouver
R.M. Wanless, FCA
Coopers & Lybrand, Vancouver
D.W. Young, CA
Ernst & Whinney, Vancouver

PREFACE

In the past two decades, the complexion of the Canadian corporate world has undergone rapid and far-reaching changes. With these changes, traditional internal controls have undergone a metamorphosis. Technological impacts have left many managers uncertain how to maintain adequate internal control within their firms.

In the past, internal control meant such things as cash management, maintenance of an audit trail, separation of duties and use of authorizing signatures to curtail possibly unacceptable activities of employees. While such controls are still desirable, some of them are becoming obsolete or are being altered by evolving computer technology.

This study serves four principal purposes. First, it gathered information from Canada's largest companies, allowing for a depiction of "state-of-the-art" internal control in the Canadian environment — an empirical examination of internal control in Canadian corporations had not been undertaken previously. This study surveyed the top 608 Canadian corporations at three management levels — chief financial officers, internal audit managers and data processing managers — and interviewed four management levels.

Second, this study provides a major database based on the examination of three management levels' responses to questions and through the grouping of responses by industry classification, size of company and whether companies are within regulated industries.

Third, the survey of the three management levels examined the roles and internal control responsibilities of individuals within the organization. Although the concerns of various management levels do sometimes overlap, the emphasis placed on particular aspects of internal control differ significantly. Those differences are documented and compared statistically across management groups.

Fourth, computerized information systems represent the most significant recent technological change within firms. With the introduction and use of these systems, new internal controls have become mandatory, altering the internal control systems of corporations as well as the roles of both internal and external auditors. This study inquires whether this change has been fully dealt with by the corporations and the two groups of auditors.

The study was enthusiastically supported by the managers who participated. The managers interviewed gave freely of valuable hours, in some instances spending two to three hours with the researchers. Hundreds of other managers participated by carefully completing questionnaires and providing an exceptionally high response rate. The researchers thank all those individuals who, for purposes of confidentiality, must remain anonymous. Without their assistance, these results could not have been attained.

The study came into existence through the support of the Canadian Institute of Chartered Accountants (CICA) and the Society of Management Accountants of Canada (SMAC). Without their funding, a study of this scope would not be possible. The researchers, therefore, are indebted to those two organizations.

Our advisory group, composed of representatives of the CICA, the SMAC, public accountants, corporate management, and academia, has provided support in several ways. Its members read the study in its various forms and attended meetings. They also made suggestions about all stages of the study that indicated a sensitivity to both the study's requirements and the respondents' time. Their interest and support has provided encouragement to the researchers from the initial stages of the project to its completion. We thank Daniel Armishaw, Director of Research, SMAC, and Ron Salole, Senior Research Studies Manager, CICA, for their contributions to our study. We thank the individual advisory group members: David Blazouske, MBA, FCA, RIA, FSMAC, of Concordia University; Michael Gibbins, PhD, CA, of University of Alberta; John Podmore, RIA, of Westcoast Transmission Ltd.; Roderick Wanless, FCA of Coopers & Lybrand; and Donald Young, CA of Ernst & Whinney.

We also wish to acknowledge the assistance of R.R. Stone, President, Financial Executives Institute Canada, Vancouver Chapter, and Bev Harrison of Arthur Andersen & Co., who, although not on the advisory committee, also provided invaluable assistance in securing interview subjects.

We have had the help of several research assistants over the course of this project as well as seed money provided from Simon Fraser University President's Research Grant. We thank: Joanne Clark, Brad Gamble, Brian Hawrysh, D. J. Sandhu and Michael Wright. Also, Jean Last typed and retyped various drafts of this study and never complained once.

Finally, our families claim that they still recognize us after many months of neglect. We thank them for their support and loyalty.

Lois D. Etherington, Ph.D.   Irene M. Gordon, Ph.D.

Chapter 1

THE RESEARCH STUDY: NEED AND MAJOR FINDINGS

Internal control deals with the processes and practices by which the management of an organization attempts to ensure that approved and appropriate decisions are made and activities carried out. It is also aimed at detecting errors and preventing officers and employees from engaging in proscribed and inappropriate activities. Growth in the size of organizations, their complexity and public sensitivity to corporate decisions has resulted in a major renewal of interest in the subject of internal control. The recent recession and a "quiet revolution in the recognition of the relationship between internal control practices and good management," (Mautz, et al., 1980, p. 1) have made this topic of even greater concern to business management and academics alike.

This study examines internal control in Canadian corporations, primarily from a management perspective, with the objective of gaining a better understanding of Canadian business practices for establishing, monitoring, and evaluating internal control systems. This study was not intended to examine internal control from the perspective of the external auditor. The external auditor and the audit committee perspective, while important to the internal control environment, has been examined in detail elsewhere in the literature (see Chapter 3) and, therefore, was not investigated here.

NEED FOR A CANADIAN STUDY

The Foreign Corrupt Practices Act (FCPA), a major regulatory mechanism for monitoring the management of US corporations, was passed in the United States in 1977, producing a burgeoning American interest in internal control. That interest resulted in increased attempts to define internal control, enlarged internal audit departments and the documentation of steps taken to achieve and secure adequate internal control. Although a popular misconception is to view US and Canadian business environments as being the same — and there are clearly many similarities — there are, nonetheless, substantial differences. Government regulations and practices differ, as do the markets, degree of competition and the labour environments. Although provisions of the FCPA apply to Canadian corporations that are subsidiaries of US parents or have US subsidiaries, it would be invalid *prima facie* to assume that internal control measures implemented in American firms would be substantially the same as those in Canadian corporations.

The recession of the early 1980s was another impetus for firms to examine their business practices, prompting an increased interest in internal control. The connection between good internal control and good management is widely recognized, although individual components of each have resisted precise definition.

The recently increased dependence on computers for operational effectiveness and financial reporting has greatly increased internal control risks. This is compounded by a shortage of adequately trained data processing and internal audit personnel who have knowledge of data processing systems. There has been some acknowledgement of this problem in the professional auditing literature but, as yet, it is being comparatively unaddressed in management literature and research.

It is apparent from the literature that there is no consensus on even a definition of internal control. The auditor's definition and perspective are the most thoroughly documented to date. These are, however, not necessarily applicable to managers, because theirs is a much broader perspective. There is also considerable evidence that disagreement exists among those in different positions within firms over the precise definition. Up to now the management perspective has been substantially unaddressed, except for three US studies (Mautz, et al., 1980, 1981 and 1983). In Canada, this is the first study concerned with managements' views on internal control.

MAJOR FINDINGS

In a short summary, it is difficult to do justice to the depth of the findings of this research. We attempt, nevertheless, to provide a broad listing of some of our major findings of this study to whet the appetite for examination of the more complete results and recommendations.

1. Canadian managers seemed to have little difficulty in defining internal control as a broad concept. From this perspective, internal control was found to encompass accounting, management and operational controls, including such factors as organizational structure, quality of personnel and management, delegation of responsibility commensurate with authority, and effective and efficient management.

2. Internal control is viewed as important and significant by corporate management, with activities at all managerial levels seen as the domain of internal control. Responsibility for internal control was widely shared among managerial levels, requiring communication and cooperation from many to ensure effective operation.

3. There is great diversity within Canadian corporations. Although major trends are identifiable, widely differing practices are found, even within size and industry groupings. It is, therefore, difficult to establish a set of uniform criteria for testing the adequacy of internal control in a specific company.

4. There appears to be a need for a more formal examination of internal control risks in some companies. While in the minority, a substantial number of corporate executives were deeply concerned about the lack of such inquiry or cost-benefit analysis in their companies.

5. Internal control of computerized information systems is the most pressing internal control problem at present and involving all levels of management. The concern of data processing managers, and their desire for more interaction with the departments they serve and with internal audit, was also well-documented.

6. Many respondents expressed a desire for a more formal specification of systems and of their own responsibilities within those systems. Communication about goals, objectives and performance evaluation criteria was viewed as an important feature, both where it existed and where it was lacking.

7. The type of industry was found to influence a number of corporate internal control practices.

8. Internal audit was viewed as a major component of internal control by the 80 percent of firms having an internal audit function. The role of the external auditor was less important by comparison, although external audit did play a major role in reporting on internal control to the board of directors.

9. All managerial levels identified significant problems with the audit of computerized systems. Both internal and external audits were assessed as wanting in this area. Internal control and audit of finance and accounting areas were well established and competently carried out, but internal control and audit of computerized activities were less well defined.

ORGANIZATION OF THE STUDY

The second chapter of this report discusses the study's objectives and the research methods employed. The third chapter outlines the literature concerned with internal control and also references recent publications on internal control aspects of data processing. The fourth chapter provides interview results, presenting the perspectives of chief executive officers, chief financial officers, internal audit managers and data processing managers.

The next two chapters provide a detailed examination of the questionnaire results. Chapter 5 outlines the responses of each of the three groups. Statistical analyses are presented that test for the effects of company size and industry classification. Chapter 6 compares data for questions asked of two or more groups. The results of statistical tests are provided that analyze the relationships between groups, as well as partitions across the groups for firm size and industry classification.

Summary and conclusions are covered in Chapter 7. The eighth chapter lists recommendations that are supported by the interview and questionnaire findings.

Chapter 2

OBJECTIVES AND RESEARCH METHODS

OBJECTIVES OF THE STUDY

The initial impetus for the study came from several sources. The first was a long-standing research interest in the subject of internal control, and in the systems used by management to communicate and achieve corporate objectives. Internal control as a cooperative endeavour, exhibiting organizational interdependencies between management levels and across managerial groups, indicated that an investigation of organizational structure and different responsibilities should be carried out.

A major objective of the study was to determine actual corporate practice by collecting empirical evidence and documentation. Previous literature, other than that from the external auditor's perspective, had been largely normative in nature. Another impetus for the study centred around the computer revolution and its impact on the organization. Ascertaining managerial concerns about the effect of computerization and attendant risks, therefore, also became an important portion of the enquiry. A summary of the objectives is presented in Exhibit I, followed by an elaboration of each objective. The rationale for the objectives is discussed in this chapter and also in Chapter 3, where previous literature on internal control is reviewed.

Exhibit I

OBJECTIVES OF THE STUDY

I. To gather data about the state of the art of internal control in Canadian corporations and to prepare a data base.

II. To explore management's understanding and definition of internal control.

    A. To define "management" for the purposes of this study.

    B. To elicit control definitions of managers.

    C. To determine what management deems the objectives of internal control to be.
- To explore understanding of "accounting control".
- To explore understanding of "managerial control".
- To compare management's definitions with the CICA definition.

III. Assessing responsibility for the internal control system.

    A. To determine who designs the systems, approves them, maintains them, evaluates their effectiveness, and authorizes system changes.

  B. To identify lines of responsibility for reporting effectiveness of internal control from the management perspective.
     To determine who reports to:
     - Financial management.
     - Senior management.
     - The board or audit committees.

IV. To identify and investigate internal control problems from the perspective of:
    - Chief financial officers.
    - Data processing or systems managers.
    - Internal auditors.

V. Identification of perceived risk factors.
   A. To compare risk factors as perceived by different management levels as:
      - General risk factors.
      - Industry specific risk factors.
   B. To rank risk factors in order of importance and to determine whether management distinguishes between preventive and detective internal control factors.

VI. Computerized systems.
    A. To identify management's perceptions of risk.
    B. To inquire whether proliferation of executive desk-top terminals poses any increased internal control risk.
    C. To identify risks (if any) from the increased use of microcomputers.

VII. To determine the effect of the US Foreign Corrupt Practices Act upon firms which are subsidiaries of US corporations.

VIII. To contrast and compare the Canadian internal control environment with that found in the United States in an earlier study.

IX. To provide recommendations about internal control practices.

I. Fact Gathering from a Management Perspective

In Canada, little empirical evidence existed about what companies do to achieve internal control. This study provides a large database for gaining a better understanding of internal control in Canadian businesses.

The study is from management's viewpoint because it is management who is primarily responsible for establishing and enforcing good internal control. An initial understanding of the subject relies in part on the background and perceptions of those who formulate and implement the corporate policies that comprise internal control. Focussing on the managerial role in the delineation of internal control can answer many questions such as why certain activities are carefully regulated while other tasks receive less emphasis. Also, if good internal controls are related to good management, then adequate recognition of the link between the role of various management levels and their specific responsibilities would contribute to understanding this interactive endeavour. The managerial focus also provides a more balanced perspective because, to date, most attention has been focussed on internal control from the perspective of external accountants. For that reason, external auditors were not surveyed or interviewed.

II. To Explore Management's Understanding and Definition of Internal Control

A. *Definition of Management for the Purposes of this Study*

In undertaking this particular objective, a decision had to be made concerning the composition of "management." The CICA defines management as "those who have authority and responsibility for planning, directing and controlling the activities of an enterprise." (*CICA Handbook*, Paragraph 5205.02). That definition, however, does not identify specific office holders and, by implicitly including the board of directors, specifically excludes only shareholders. Members of boards of directors, however, are not commonly believed to be company management, unless they hold dual positions.

Although all senior, middle and lower management are involved in some aspects of internal control, the cost of interviewing and surveying all management levels would have been prohibitive, in terms of both time and money. Although the vice president of operations and the production manager, for example, are involved in enforcing internal controls for their areas, these individuals are included only peripherally in the establishment of internal control procedures. The primary guideline selected for this study, therefore, was to include individuals who are most directly responsible for internal control procedures and their ultimate enforcement. The principal representatives of management for the purposes of this project were defined as the chief executive officer and the chief financial officer.

Two other management groups were interviewed and surveyed — data processing managers and internal audit managers. Neither is regarded as senior management, but these officers implement and monitor internal control and, particularly for internal audit, are reporters to senior management and audit committees on the health of internal control. Although these groups remain outside the definition of top management, an examination of their role in the internal control system served to illuminate discrepancies between the perspectives of senior and middle management.

B. *Internal Control Definitions*

In Canada, internal control itself has remained undefined by management, other than peripherally by the Financial Executives Institute (1981). In one US study (Mautz and Winjum, 1981), managers were requested to define internal control, a process that led to the conclusion that internal control was composed of two distinct components — accounting control and managerial control. Thus, the definition of internal control will be refined based on those findings, and discussed with references to those two areas.

While the *CICA Handbook* defines internal control in Section 5205, the definition had not previously been presented specifically to financial management, other than those who are chartered accountants. This study would inquire whether senior corporate managers agree with the *Handbook* definition.

C. *To Examine Management's Internal Control Objectives*

In determining management's perspective of internal control, it is first necessary to understand how management specifies the objectives of internal control. If a cross-section of managers were inconsistent in their delineation of the objectives of internal control, as was found in an earlier US study (Mautz, et al., 1980), then these inconsistencies could lead to an understanding that internal control objectives have characteristics specific to particular industries.

III. Assessing Responsibility for the Internal Control System

A. *Responsibility Levels*

An internal management perspective should entail an examination of the internal control system from the organizational construct of assignment of responsibility for the system's components. That inquiry would determine management practices concerning responsibility for the design and approval of the system and, subsequently, responsibility for maintenance, evaluation and authorization of changes to the system. Clearly, to produce an effective system, definite responsibility for various components should be specified.

B. *To Whom is Effectiveness Reported?*

In any internal control study, the system's effectiveness must be investigated and reported. In assessing system effectiveness, management described their corporation's assignment of responsibility for reporting on the system's effectiveness, as well as to whom effectiveness was reported.

IV. Identification and Investigation of Internal Control from Varying Perspectives

The perspectives considered were those of the chief financial officers, the data processing or systems managers, and the internal auditors. These groups were selected as being the managers most representative in establishing, maintaining, monitoring and identifying problem areas in their internal control systems.

V. Identification of Perceived Risk Factors

A. *Comparison of Risk Factors*

Previous works (Mautz, et al., 1980, 1981) found that the higher the responding manager's level in the firm, the lower the risk element was perceived to be. Comparisons of various firms' managers' perceptions of risk were intended to determine if a similar situation exists in Canada. Comparisons were then made between firms' perceived risk factors to determine whether general risks could be isolated from industry-specific risks.

Risk factors are thought to be addressed by one or both of preventive or detective internal control procedures (*CICA Handbook*, Para. 5205.05). This study investigated whether management distinguishes between these two types of internal control.

B. *Ranking of Risk Factors*

Once risk factors were identified, managers were asked to rank them. Such a ranking would assist internal auditors or managers in addressing their system weaknesses.

While general risks can be identified and ranked, it is difficult to assign monetary values to them, because the amounts in question are highly enterprise-and-situation specific. The issue of control must, however, be dealt with from the perspective of limited corporate resources, leading to the necessity to rank controls in some order depending on "exposure" or business risk[1], such as the following:

> Erroneous record-keeping, unacceptable accounting, business interruption, erroneous management decisions, fraud and embezzlement, statutory sanctions, excessive costs, loss or destruction of assets, competitive disadvantage, shareholder suits over alleged failures in accountability, loss of public confidence, public embarrassment, liquidity problems, excessive dependency on scarce resources, and misuses of assets and other corporate resources (as quoted in Fisher, 1978, p.354).[2]

A ranking of exposure risks, undertaken in this research, would indicate, for example, that more control dollars should be spent to control the highest risk factors.

A cost-benefit analysis of the internal control system would seem to be an extension of ranking the risk factors. Usually, it is argued that controls should be implemented whenever the benefit exceeds the cost. Two problems arise, however, when undertaking any cost-benefit analysis. There are problems associated with measuring the costs, because they are highly situation specific and depend on the organization's size, type of management and existing control systems. In addition, the determination of benefits achieved by specific controls is an extremely complex issue.

One study (Fisher, 1978) found that the benefits of various aspects of an internal control system are difficult to estimate except where inadequate controls have led to specific losses. This finding was supported by the American Institute of Certified Public Accountants (AICPA) Special Advisory Committee on Internal Accounting Control which, in limiting the scope of its study concluded "significant aspects of costs and of risks or benefits cannot be reduced to monetary terms without using subjective business judgment" (1979, p. 3). The area of losses arising from lack of internal control in electronic data processing, for example, is just beginning to be documented in business literature. Since this area of internal control is changing rapidly, and is in an exploratory stage, it was anticipated by the researchers that quantification would not prove feasible.

VI. Computerized Systems

Within the past two decades, computerized systems have proliferated, creating the need for controls specifically designed for computerized data processing. Previous studies of internal control have failed to address, on a large scale, management's assessments of computer-associated risk. This study was designed to assess and rank risks of computerized systems.

Several other areas of concern with respect to computer utilization were also examined: problem areas directly related to the use of mainframe computers; problems due to the increasing presence of terminals on the desks of many executives, which greatly increases access to data bases; and the impact, of microcomputers on internal control.

VII. US Foreign Corrupt Practices Act

An additional objective was to determine the effect of the FCPA on firms that are subsidiaries of US corporations. Discussions with some Canadian corporate officers brought out the fact that the requirements of the FCPA — that all publicly traded firms, whether engaged in foreign business or not, report on the efficacy of their internal control systems and document steps taken to obtain and maintain good internal control — had resulted in substantially increased attention to compliance with those provisions[3]. For that reason, increased attention to internal control was thought to be widespread in Canadian firms subject to US reporting standards.

VIII. To Compare and Contrast Canadian and US Internal Control Environments

The Canadian internal control environment will be compared to and contrasted with that found in earlier US studies (Mautz, et al., 1980, 1981, 1983). This study extends the Mautz studies, exploring a number of aspects not addressed in those earlier works, but will, nevertheless, provide valuable comparisons between the two countries.

IX. To Provide Recommendations About Internal Control Practices

Finally, recommendations will be made based on both interview and question-naire findings. Although these recommendations cannot be construed to be prescriptive for a particular corporation, they can provide a useful guide for managers interested in examining the internal control practices within their firms. Both internal and external auditors may find the recommendations of similar interest.

RESEARCH METHODS

The study began with a literature search that found little conceptual work, few references beyond articles primarily of normative work designed for a profes-sional auditing audience and little empirical work other than three recent US publications (Mautz, et al., 1980, 1981, 1983). The research was designed to provide a large database from which it would be possible to examine the practice of internal control in Canada's largest corporations. Data were collected in two distinct phases — by interview and then by questionnaire.

The subjects for the study comprised the complete set of the largest corpora-tions in the country. They were all the companies from the *Financial Post* "Top 500" listing, plus 108 of the largest financial institutions, which are not included in the "Top 500" listing, bringing the total to 608 Canadian corporations. First, interviews were conducted with four management levels of selected corporations at their head offices, followed by questionnaire preparation and a survey of three management levels at all 608 corporations.

The Interview Phase

Interviews of corporate officers — chief executive officers, chief financial officers, internal audit managers and data processing managers — were conducted during the summer of 1983. The interviews had several objectives:

- To gain an appreciation of the way internal control was viewed by Canadian managers and how their perceptions might differ from those in the published literature.
- To identify the internal control practices used in the companies.
- To explore differences, if any, between the internal control environments of Canada and the United States.
- To address issues of internal control that managers found to be a problem.

The interview results were then used to develop a set of uniquely Canadian questionnaires that would address the topic of internal control.

To represent a wide variety of industries and environmental influences, the six companies chosen for this phase of the project included a retailer, an oil and gas pipeline firm, a holding company whose major subsidiaries were manufacturing firms, a mining company, a petroleum firm and a public utility. Three of the firms — the utility, the pipeline and the petroleum company, reported to Canadian regulatory agencies.

The combined assets of the firms interviewed for the 1982 reporting period ranged from $3.8 million to more than $2.6 billion. The 1982 net income figures for the six firms were split evenly into two groups, with half showing increased profits and half indicating decreased profits compared to 1981. Two firms had US parents and one firm had both a US subsidiary and a British parent, and two other companies had subsidiaries located in the United States. One firm in the sample had neither a foreign parent nor a foreign subsidiary. This composition allowed the interviewers to incorporate questions on the US Foreign Corrupt Practices Act.

Management styles varied in the six firms. Two of the firms were highly centralized, with almost all decisions being made through head office. On the other end of the spectrum, one firm had a decentralized management style. The other three firms were mixed, with some management functions centralized at head office while others were maintained within corporate divisions or groups.

The officers from the six companies included three chief executive officers, six chief financial officers, six internal audit managers and five data processing managers. All of the interviews were conducted at the head offices of the companies in Toronto and Vancouver. Interview times ranged from 45 minutes to two and one-half hours. The interviews were structured, with specific questions developed to act as guides to the interview format (see Appendix A). The interviewees, however, expanded considerably in their answers, and much lively discussion ensued.

Interview questions varied, depending on the organizational level of the interviewee, but centred around several themes:
• Definitions of internal control.
• Level of control consciousness in the interviewee's firm.
• Key elements of internal control.
• Actions taken by the interviewee to strengthen the internal control environment.
• The role of internal audit.
• The role of external audit.
• Internal control risks.
• The corporate code of conduct.
• The effect (if any) of the US Foreign Corrupt Practices Act.

Themes that centred around the internal control of computerized information systems were:
• The role of data processing in the corporation and its place in the organizational structure.
• Internal control aspects of electronic data processing.
• Internal audit involvement.
• Risks.
• External audit's role in internal control of data processing.

The Questionnaire Phase

Building on the results of the interviews, the researchers prepared a separate questionnaire for each of three target groups: (1) chief financial officers, (2) internal audit managers and (3) data processing managers.

Some topics and specific questions were addressed to all three groups, allowing for comparison across organizational levels. Other topics and specific questions applied mainly to one or two particular managerial levels. The three samples provided an extensive set of data, giving a broad perspective of internal control in Canadian corporations.

A number of factors were considered in determining the areas to be investigated by the questionnaires. While an earlier study by Mautz, et al., in 1980, which surveyed chief financial officers, was valuable, the present study materially extends this work.

Important considerations were concerns that managers expressed during the interviews. It was thought important to determine, through the questionnaires, whether those concerns were prevalent among all Canadian firms. Other issues, such as definitional questions, which appeared to be of earlier concern, seemed to have been resolved quite conclusively in the minds of Canadian managers as indicated by the Financial Executives Institute Canada in 1981 and again by the interview findings. Definitional issues were, therefore, not investigated any further in the questionnaire phase. Some areas concerned with questions about detailed internal control procedures such as cash management, accounting and reporting schedules, charts of accounts, bank reconciliations, etc., were not included because those were thought to be well-defined in practice. The well-established nature of these controls was attested to by the advisory group, several of whom had expertise in the area of Canadian practice, and was also supported by the findings of a US study (Mautz, et al., 1980).

Demographic data were collected from all managers. Other topics examined by the questionnaires were:

• Communication of internal control policies.
• Objectives of internal control.
• Responsibility for internal control systems.
• Reporting and monitoring relationships.
• The role of internal audit.
• Internal control of computerized systems.
• Risk·assessment, including evaluation of strengths as well as weaknesses.
• The role and perception of external audit.
• Effect (if any) of the US Foreign Corrupt Practices Act.

Following the initial questionnaire formulation, the researchers met with members of the advisory group and incorporated several of their recommendations. Before the questionnaires were printed, a pre-test of the three questionnaires was conducted with the executives of a few corporations headquartered in Vancouver.

A total of 1,824 questionnaires was mailed to the 608 Canadian corporations. Questionnaires were first mailed out in late 1983, with a follow-up mailing in early 1984. For both mailings, each company received copies of the three questionnaires, as well as a letter from the Canadian Institute of Chartered Accountants (CICA) and the Society of Management Accountants of Canada (SMAC) (see Appendix B for copies of the questionnaires and letters) asking the designated managers to complete the questionnaires themselves rather than delegating the task to a subordinate. Nonrespondents to the first mailing were mailed the second package, which also included a letter from the researchers.

The first mailing was directed to the chief financial officer, internal audit manager and data processing manager; the second was sent directly to the chief financial officer for distribution to the appropriate managers, who could not be identified by name.

Table 2.1 indicates the responses received for the first and second mailings. The combined response rate averaged 44.6 percent, which was minimally reduced when unusable responses were deducted. This rate is higher than the 20-40 percent response rates normally expected for mailed questionnaires (Kerlinger, 1973), and is considerably higher than the rate of 33 percent reported in an earlier survey of 2,000 chief financial officers of American companies (Mautz, et al., 1980).

TABLE 2.1

QUESTIONNAIRE RESPONSE RATE BY MANAGERIAL POSITION

| | Managerial Position | | | | | |
| | Chief Financial Officer | | Internal Audit Manager | | Data Processing Manager | |
	#	%	#	%	#	%
Sample size	608	100.0	608	100.0	608	100.0
Total usable responses	263	43.3	232	38.2	268	44.1
Responses:						
First mailing	210	34.5	198	32.6	199	32.7
Second mailing	59	9.7	66	10.8	82	13.5
Total responses	269	44.2	264	43.4	281	46.2

The responses are not necessarily from the same companies, because all three officers from the same firm did not necessarily respond. A minority of companies do not have an internal audit function and, therefore, no internal audit manager; other companies, also a minority, have decentralized data processing without a designated data processing manager. Given the large sample size and an excellent response rate, however, data from the three groups enabled comparisons to be made across groups.

The second mailing also produced a favourable response rate, which increased the response rate total by 11.3 percent — normally, a second mailing elicits approximately a further 10 percent response rate.

Table 2.2 shows that the underlying population is well represented by the sample. Only two categories — holding companies and food processing firms — appear to have fewer firms represented than would be ideal. The actual questionnaires listed only eight industry categories and "Other"; therefore, it is likely that a respondent in a firm with many divisions or component parts designated the firm as one of the listed categories and avoided "Other." This explanation is particularly likely for holding companies that undertake a variety of activities.

Frequency counts and percentage calculations were made for absolute frequency, relative frequency and adjusted frequency. To test whether certain aspects of internal control were affected by industry characteristics, statistical tests by size were also performed. Although the sample companies were, by definition, Canada's largest, they were asked to classify themselves as small, medium or large. The small and medium (totalling 34.4 percent) were grouped together and their data compared to those of large companies. Responses were also analyzed by industry to test whether some internal control practices appeared more prevalent in some industries. The data were subjected to statistical tests and significant differences found were reported.

Interview results are reported in Chapter 4 and questionnaire results are in Chapters 5 and 6; Chapter 6 provides data for results of comparisons across managerial groups and countries.

TABLE 2.2

INDUSTRY REPRESENTATION BY RESPONDENT GROUP

Industry	Total Number of Firms by Group (#)	Percent of the Total (%)	Chief Financial Officer		Internal Audit Manager		Data Processing Manager	
			Frequency Count in Sample (#)	Percentage of Sample (%)	Frequency Count in Sample (#)	Percentage of Sample (%)	Frequency Count in Sample (#)	Percentage of Sample (%)
Manufacturing	169	27.8	93	36.8	78	33.6	87	32.5
Financial Services	108	17.8	46	18.2	48	20.7	46	17.2
Petroleum and Energy	42	6.9	20	7.9	18	7.6	26	9.7
Holding Companies	39	6.4	2	0.1	2	0.9	3	1.1
Retailing	37	6.1	11	4.3	16	6.9	23	8.6
Food Processing	34	5.6	3	1.2	5	2.2	8	3.0
Mining	26	4.3	8	3.2	6	2.6	8	3.0
Forestry	24	3.9	10	4.0	5	2.2	8	3.0
Utilities	23	3.8	17	6.7	19	8.2	15	5.6
Wholesalers	19	3.1	12	4.7	5	2.2	4	1.5
Transportation	15	2.5	6	2.4	10	4.3	12	4.5
Insurance	14	2.3	3	1.2	7	3.0	4	1.5
Unions/Marketing Boards	14	2.3	3	1.2	3	1.3	1	0.4
Construction	11	1.8	6	2.4	2	0.9	6	2.2
Development and Real Estate	10	1.6	3	1.2	4	1.7	4	1.5
Other	23	3.8	10	4.0	4	1.7	13	4.9
Total	608	100.0	253	99.5*	232	100.0	268	100.2*

* Due to rounding error.

Note: The category of "Other" was composed of firms in the fields of telecommunications, hotels, restaurant chains, food services, publishing and broadcasting.

Footnotes

[1] As Fisher (1978, p. 354) points out in her footnote: "The literature in risk management, while not traditionally considered to be part of control literature, offers a similar approach. See for instance, Rabel, W.H. and Hughes, C.E., 'Risk Management,' *Journal of Accounting, Auditing and Finance*, Fall, 1977, pp. 83-88."

[2] "W.C. Mair, D.R. Wood and K.W. Davis, *Computer Control & Audit*, Institute of Internal Auditors, Inc., Altamonte Springs, Fla., pp. 11-12, list the first nine of these business exposures" (Fisher, 1978, p. 354).

[3] In 1983 The Business Accounting and Foreign Trade Simplification Act was introduced in the US Senate. The proposed legislation would have resulted in changes to some of the reporting requirements of The Foreign Corrupt Practices Act (AICPA, April, 1983, p. 12). This legislation did not pass both houses of Congress during the last legislative sitting. However, it is anticipated that the bill will be re-introduced in the near future.

Chapter 3

LITERATURE SURVEY

Previous literature dealing with the subject of internal control has been some-what diverse. Some areas, such as internal control from the perspective of external auditors, have been addressed quite thoroughly, while others have remained largely unexamined. This chapter reviews major works and identifies some gaps in the existing literature. Where this study has been designed to address perceived shortcomings in the literature, the authors will comment briefly on its expected contribution.

The literature will be reviewed below in the following categories:
- Definitions of internal control.
- The relationship of ethics and the corporate code of conduct to internal control.
- The role of the audit committee.
- The US Foreign Corrupt Practices Act of 1977 and its influence on internal control.
- Recent American empirical studies on internal control.
- The effect of the computerization of information systems on internal control.

INTERNAL CONTROL DEFINITIONS

The historical background of the term "internal control" represents the development of a definition that was in response to a need. External auditors were the primary users and beneficiaries of the original definition and the clarifications that followed. While this development has generally been satisfactory from the external auditor's perspective, the resulting definition has not been particularly appropriate for other users. For example, management has often found existing definitions of internal control to be too narrow. The major definitive statements about internal control have been made by The American Institute of Certified Public Accountants (AICPA), The Canadian Institute of Chartered Accountants (CICA), and, more recently, by a US study (Mautz and Winjum, 1981) that approaches internal control from a management perspective.

Definition from an External Auditor Perspective

1. Development of the AICPA Definition
Within the history of accounting, auditing has been a dynamic area. Rules and

statements of conduct for external auditors began to appear primarily in the 1940s. The first AICPA definition of internal control was published in 1949 and still represents the broadest perspective in the public accounting literature to date:

> Internal control comprises the plan of organization and all of the coordinate methods and measures adopted within a business to safeguard its assets, check the accuracy and reliability of its accounting data, promote operational efficiency, and encourage adherence to prescribed managerial policies. This definition possibly is broader than the meaning sometimes attributed to the term. It recognizes that a "system" of internal control extends beyond those matters which relate directly to the functions of the accounting and financial departments. Such a system might include budgetary control, standard costs, periodic operating reports, statistical analyses . . . (and) training program(s) . . . It properly comprehends activities in other fields as, for example, time and motion studies which are of an engineering nature, and use of quality controls (Committee on Auditing Procedures, 1949, p. 6).

The reaction to this definition was, in part, negative. The breadth of "internal control," as defined in the 1949 report, left external auditors with seemingly endless responsibility. From a practical viewpoint, such a definition could leave auditors open to charges of failure to fulfill their responsibilities if they should fail to evaluate the adequacy of all the various aspects of internal control.

Consequently, the 1949 definition was revised in 1958, dividing internal control into administrative and accounting controls:

> Accounting controls comprise the plan of organization and all methods and procedures that are concerned mainly with, and relate directly to, the safeguarding of assets and the reliability of the financial records. They generally include such controls as the systems of authorization and approval, separation of duties concerned with record keeping and accounting reports from those concerned with operations or asset custody, physical controls over assets, and internal auditing.

> Administrative controls comprise the plan of organization and all methods and procedures that are concerned mainly with operational efficiency and adherence to managerial policies and usually relate only indirectly to the financial records. They generally include such controls as statistical analyses, time and motion studies, performance reports, employee training programs, and quality controls. (As quoted in AICPA, 1978, pp. 41-42).

The primary purpose of the 1958 restatement was to narrow the scope of the external auditor's responsibility to that of accounting controls only.

A second revision was made to the definition in 1972, distinguishing between administrative and accounting controls, with the latter even more clearly articulated than before:

Administrative control includes, but is not limited to, the plan of organization and the procedures and records that are concerned with the decision processes leading to management's authorization of transactions. Such authorization is a management function directly associated with the responsibility for achieving the objectives of the organization and is the starting point for establishing accounting control of transactions.

Accounting control comprises the plan of organization and the procedures and records that are concerned with the safeguarding of assets and the reliability of financial records and consequently are designed to provide reasonable assurance that:

a. Transactions are executed in accordance with management's general or specific authorization.
b. Transactions are recorded as necessary (1) to permit preparation of financial statements in conformity with generally accepted accounting principles or any other criteria applicable to such statements and (2) to maintain accountability for assets.
c. Access to assets is permitted only in accordance with management's authorization.
d. The recorded accountability for assets is compared with the existing assets at reasonable intervals and appropriate action is taken with respect to any differences. (As quoted in AICPA, 1978, pp. 41 and 42.)

2. The CICA Definition

The CICA also defined internal control for external auditors practising in Canada. The definition is specified in Section 5200, paragraphs .05 – .08 of the *CICA Handbook*:

.05 Internal control comprises the plan of organization and all the coordinate systems established by the management of an enterprise to assist in achieving management's objective of ensuring, as far as practical, the orderly and efficient conduct of its business, including the safeguarding of assets, the reliability of accounting records and the timely preparation of reliable financial information.

.06 Internal control within an enterprise consists of many systems each of which is designed to help management achieve its particular objectives. Each system comprises numerous internal controls, of which some are inter-dependent and others function independently. Each system, in order to be effective, must be well designed and properly operated.

.07 There is a distinction between the exercise of internal control and the determination of business policies. Even though internal control includes all the controls established by management to achieve its objectives, it does not encompass all management activities. For example, determining a sales policy is a business decision; monitoring the implementation of that policy (such as in the proper application of selling prices) is a function of internal control.

.08 An accounting system is an important element of internal control but is not in itself an internal control system. An internal control system includes comparisons, determination of discrepancies and decisions as to corrective action, as well as controls over the accounting system.

In intent, this broad-based definition is closer to the AICPA's 1949 internal control definition than to the later revised versions. The CICA did, however, in later *Handbook* sections further refine and limit the role and responsibility of external auditors. The extent of an auditor's evaluation of a firm's internal control system is specified in Section 5210, paragraphs .05 – .06 of the *CICA Handbook*.

.05 The extent of the auditor's study and evaluation of internal control is determined by his judgment as to the most efficient way of obtaining sufficient appropriate audit evidence to support the content of his report. An auditor engaged to report on financial statements, such as in a statutory audit, has no responsibility to make an examination of internal control beyond that which he makes in determining the nature, extent and timing of other auditing procedures, unless there are additional contractual requirements to the contrary.

.06 The auditor may be unable to or may choose not to rely on particular internal controls on which management relies because, for example,
(a) The control is not useful for the auditor's purposes; for internal reporting purposes management may design internal controls over the accuracy of classification, details and allocations which are not required for external reporting purposes and which therefore are not of direct concern to the auditor;
(b) the auditor is unable to apply compliance procedures . . . to gain a sufficient degree of assurance as to the effective operation of the internal control; management may, because of its physical presence and knowledge of the business, rely on direct supervision of employees. The auditor might conclude that he is unable to satisfy himself as to the effectiveness of management's supervision and he would therefore not rely on it.

This is reinforced by paragraphs .06, .10, .12, .17 and .23, in Section 5220 which state that, if auditors are going to rely on certain internal controls within a firm, they must be prepared to study and evaluate those controls for both the substantive and compliance steps of the audit. Paragraph 5, Section 5210, indicates, however, that where the auditor's examination clearly does not rely on certain controls, there is no responsibility for evaluating them. The CICA and the AICPA views are similar in that they delineate and narrow the auditor's responsibility for internal controls.

3. Commission on Auditors' Responsibilities

Many accountants and managers believe there is evidence that important areas of control would be ignored if accounting controls were singled out. For example, Fisher (1978, p. 351) states that if a concentration on accounting controls "provides a scope which is too limited for the external auditor, it will also be too limited to serve as a focal point for management control efforts." The broader nature of control has been addressed by the AICPA, Commission on Auditors' Responsibilities (1977, pp. 51-64), which pointed out that accountability includes more than proper recordkeeping and that investors have a right to know that all aspects of management are under control. These studies provide evidence of support for the inclusion of additional areas within the aegis of internal control.

Definitions from a Managerial Perspective

1. Financial Executives Institute Canada

A FEIC monograph — *Integrity in Business* — offered a broad definition of internal control from a managerial perspective:

> Internal control must extend beyond specific procedures undertaken in the accounting, financial and audit functions. In its broadest sense, the internal control system includes many other factors, such as management philosophy, organization structure, quality of personnel, delegation of responsibility with commensurate authority and segregation of duties (Financial Executives Institute Canada, 1981, p. 5).

2. Mautz and Winjum Definition of Internal Control

A US study produced a report dividing internal control into two parts: accounting control and management control (Mautz and Winjum, 1981, p. 28). As a result of testing many internal control definitions, the authors returned to the concepts of the AICPA's 1949 and 1972 definitions of internal control. Proposing to discourage the use of the term "internal control," which they considered too broad and undefined, they suggested that the 1972 AICPA definition be used when referring to accounting control and that management control be defined as it was in the comprehensive 1949 AICPA definition.

3. Society of Management Accountants of Canada

Recently, the Society of Management Accountants of Canada issued an exposure draft of a guideline addressing internal control from a managerial accounting perspective (Society of Management Accountants of Canada, 1984). The definition adopted for use in the proposed guideline is broad-based and was originally outlined by the International Federation of Accountants in their *Handbook* (1981, p. 9-41). This definition states that:

> The system of internal control is the plan of organization and all the methods and procedures adopted by the management of an entity to assist in achieving management's objective of ensuring, as far as practicable, the orderly and efficient conduct of its business, including adherence to management policies, the safeguarding of assets, the prevention and detection of fraud and error, the accuracy and completeness of the accounting records, and the timely preparation of reliable financial information. The system of internal control extends beyond those matters which relate directly to the functions of the accounting system . . .

Nonprofit Definitions of Internal Control

1. The Canadian Comprehensive Auditing Foundation

The Canadian Comprehensive Auditing Foundation (CCAF), a leader in governmental and not-for-profit auditing, has included the aspects of economy and efficiency and program effectiveness in the audit scope. Doing so recognizes that, at least in the nonprofit organization, the accomplishment of management objectives and of economy and efficiency are important aspects of the control environment of the organization. A comprehensive audit was stated to review:

> . . . financial controls, reporting attest and authority, management control, and EDP controls. Under this concept the Auditor General will report to Parliament

. . . his evaluation of the quality of the management of public funds and resources from the standpoint of economy and efficiency and of the procedures for measuring reporting of program effectiveness (Macdonell, 1979, pp. 5-9).

2. *The US Government Accounting Office*

The US Government Accounting Office (GAO), also an agency concerned with monitoring public-sector spending and compliance, has implicitly recognized the broader definition of internal control by issuing guidelines (1972) for three levels of audits: (1) financial and compliance, (2) economy and efficiency and (3) program results. The latter two audit levels are further evidence that, from a governmental perspective, internal control objectives are affected by internal management in addition to the traditional reporting of compliance.

Because there is no agreement on the definition of internal control, this study will examine which of the many possible aspects Canadian business executives include in their definitions of internal control.

Institute of Internal Auditors' Internal Control Perspective

In its 1978 *Standards for the Professional Practice of Internal Auditing*, the Institute of Internal Auditors (IIA) spelled out five objectives of the internal control function.

1. Reliability, and integrity of information.
2. Compliance with policies, plans, procedures, laws and regulations.
3. Safeguarding of assets.
4. Economical and efficient use of resources.
5. Accomplishment of established objectives and goals for operations or programs.

The IIA standards represent an extremely broad perspective of internal control, a perspective quite similar to the orientation of the Financial Executives Institute Canada as well as the nonprofit orientation.

THE RELATIONSHIP BETWEEN CORPORATE INTEGRITY AND CONTROL

Two Canadian groups — the CICA and the FEIC — have addressed the relationship between corporate integrity and internal control. The Adams Committee report (CICA, 1978) recommended CICA input for the development of guidelines for the preparation of corporate codes of conduct. In its 1981 monograph on integrity in business, the FEIC postulated that being good corporate citizens may be the only way to ensure the preservation of the free enterprise system.

One issue highlighted was the company and its ethical environment. That ethical environment was said to permeate the company's objectives, mission and obligations. The FEIC recommended that ethics should be spelled out clearly in corporate codes of conduct and that employees should be made aware of their responsibilities within that framework.

Another issue addressed was the role of internal control and its place in ensuring the ethical functioning of the firm. After defining internal control broadly, the roles of the controller, internal audit function, independent auditor, audit committee and the management report were discussed in general terms. This monograph serves to emphasize the interest in and the need for further analysis of internal control within Canadian firms.

THE ROLE OF AUDIT COMMITTEES IN INTERNAL CONTROL

The Adams Report (CICA, 1978) recommended an investigation into the role and responsibilities of audit committees. The resulting CICA research study, *Audit Committees* (1981) outlined the legislation in Canada and found that the Canada Business Corporations Act and the corporations acts in British Columbia, Manitoba, Ontario and Saskatchewan required corporations to establish an audit committee of not fewer than three directors.[1] Moreover, the statutes required that the majority of the audit committee not be officers or employees of the corporation and its affiliates.

In addition, the CICA study found that the internal control functions assigned to the audit committee were to:

1. Review problems encountered, any restriction on auditor's work, cooperation received and their findings.

2. Review the external auditor's evaluation of the company's internal control systems, and significant recommendations to management, and management's response.

3. Review organization and independence of internal auditors.

4. Follow up significant recommendations for improvement of accounting and internal control practices by the company's internal auditors.

5. Review problems and experience in completing internal audits.

6. Review goals and plans of internal audit, including nature and extent of work.

7. Monitor adherence of company officials to company's code of conduct (CICA, 1981, p. 22).

Although not all of those functions were being undertaken by audit committees in 1981, all were advocated. Because the CICA study examined the role of the audit committee in internal control, the present study does not focus on the responsibilities of the audit committee. It has, however, researched corporate reporting structures and relationships to the audit committee within the corporation.

US FOREIGN CORRUPT PRACTICES ACT

An important influence on the concept of internal control was the US Foreign Corrupt Practices Act. Passed by US Congress in 1977, the FCPA prohibits payments to foreign officials, parties or candidates to obtain business, and also requires accurate recordkeeping and effective systems of internal control of all publicly-held companies, whether or not the firms are involved in foreign business. For the first time, the FCPA subjected public companies and their officers and employees to civil liability and criminal prosecution under federal securities laws for not having adequate systems of internal control. Because the act failed to define explicitly what the criteria would be for determining whether an internal control system was adequate, both corporate and public accounting attention was directed, in response to the act, to the examination of existing internal control systems and the documentation of compliance attempts.[2]

One result of the FCPA was that almost all large accounting firms undertook studies of internal control (Fletcher, 1981, p. 43) which frequently ended with the publication of guides on the evaluation of computerized systems rather than more meaningful definitions of internal control.

MAUTZ STUDIES

Two major US works on internal control, prompted by the passage of the FCPA, have been studies by Mautz, et al., (1980 and 1981) The first exploratory study (1980) was designed to examine the state of the art of internal control in US corporations. Commissioned by the Financial Executives Institute (FEI), seven researchers with varied academic expertise provided an interdisciplinary approach. Interviews were conducted with senior managements of 50 US companies, after which questionnaires were mailed to chief financial officers of the *Fortune* 1,000 companies plus additional FEI members. The survey provided previously unavailable information about the perspectives of managers and about corporate internal control practices.

In the second study (Mautz and Winjum, 1981), the researchers conducted seminars across the country with senior management personnel, with the goal of developing a set of criteria that management could use to assist in evaluating their own internal control systems. The resulting criteria were broad-based and general.

A system of internal control was defined as consisting of four components:

1. The internal control environment within the organization.

2. A process of risk analysis to identify and evaluate the internal control risks faced by the organization.

3. The selection of appropriate internal control practices and procedures to meet the internal control risks identified and evaluated in (2).

4. A monitoring procedure to determine and report the effectiveness with which internal control procedures accomplish their intended purpose (Mautz and Winjum, 1981, p. 19).

Before a firm can be reasonably assured of having an adequate system, each of the components listed must be broken down into situation-specific elements. While these criteria are somewhat helpful as a general model, a model for a particular firm would require a thorough examination of that firm's individual characteristics.

INTERNAL CONTROL AND COMPUTERIZED SYSTEMS

Internal control of manual accounting systems has had several hundred years to evolve into a defined and standard discipline (Lee, 1971), but the same claim cannot be made for computerized environments. Indeed, the media are quick to acquaint their audiences with the details of some of the more spectacular losses due to the failure or inadequacy of controls surrounding computerized systems.[3]

A major category of literature on the topic of internal control of computerized systems is a normative approach to auditors and management — guidelines on "how to" ensure the integrity of their computer systems and avoid associated risks.

A Normative Approach

The 1970s saw computer expansion in many facets of the business world, including sensitive areas such as banking, payroll records and customer accounts, and in small and medium businesses as well as in large corporations.

Two of the first internal control publications to appear in Canada, *Computer Control Guidelines* (CICA, 1970) and *Computer Audit Guidelines* (CICA, 1975), were published by the CICA as a result of the pressure on external auditors created by a changing computer environment. Most of the suggestions made in these guides have also been made elsewhere in articles (Mastromano, 1982a; 1982b) textbooks (Porter and Perry, 1981) and guides published in other countries (Jenkins and Pinkney, 1978). Public accounting firms have also produced a number of publications directed at assisting management in evaluating systems controls within their firms (for example, Coopers and Lybrand, 1977 and 1983; and Catania, Dick, and Silverman, 1980). Some of the standard suggestions have included:
- Separation of duties that serve as checks on the computer system.
- Use of back-up files.
- Documenting changes to the system or programs.
- Requiring authorization for all program changes.
- Sign-on controls for sensitive data.
- Controlling access to the physical computer facilities.
- Maintaining and testing disaster plans.

One particularly sensitive area addressed in the literature is the problem of risk assessment and who should be responsible for it. Perry (1983, p. 33) recommended that personnel involved in risk analysis of computerized systems should hold the following positions, providing varying experience and expertise:
- EDP operations management.
- Systems programming.
- Security officer.
- Data base administrator.
- Project personnel.
- Users of the application system.

Where the potential benefits outweigh the costs, the risks should be investigated.

Foh (1983) recommended the external auditor as an independent third party who is in a unique position to examine a proposed computer system, in a pre-implementation audit, to determine whether the controls on the system will ensure reliability of information. The works by Foh (1983) and Perry (1983) are representative of the large body of normative prescriptions for controlling computerized information systems.

The internal control of distributed computer systems is now receiving the attention once given to mainframe computers and associated control problems (for example see Brown, 1983; Fogler and Sanderson, 1983; and Dewar, 1983). Suggestions on how to minimize risks are generally the same as those made to maintain integrity for a mainframe computer operation without the subsidiary operations.

Empirical Research on Computerized Systems and Internal Control

Although most literature has focussed on external auditors and has concentrated on ways to help management carry out their responsibilities, only one study to date has attempted to document the concerns of senior management in the context of computerized information systems (Mautz, et al, 1983). Collecting data first through a series of interviews in 12 companies, two CPA firms and two computer-vendor firms and, second, through a series of management seminars, this US study addressed the problems associated with computer dependency. Ten issues were found to be of significant importance:

1. Organizational location of responsibility for information systems.
2. Assignment of responsibilities among all parties concerned with the planning, acquisition, use and control of information systems.
3. Assimilation of the information systems function into the company.
4. Organization of the information systems function.
5. Cost control over information systems development and operating activities.
6. Measuring the efficiency and effectiveness of the information systems function.
7. Assuring reliable computer security.
8. Effective use of internal audit function.
9. Computer use for competitive advantage.
10. Establishment and maintenance of senior management control (Mautz, et al., 1983, p. 9).

The main proviso of this exploratory US study was to note that the resolution of management problems with control over computers tends to be company specific and that their report could give only general guidance.[4]

After a comprehensive literature review, we reached two major conclusions. Many issues either (1) have been widely discussed but not empirically examined in a broad-based manner or (2) have been examined in a US context but not in a Canadian one. This study was designed to correct these deficiencies.

Footnotes

[1] In 1982, one year after the CICA audit committee study, Alberta passed a new corporations act. This legislation also requires the establishment of an audit committee of not less than three directors where a majority of members must not be officers or employees of the corporation or its affiliates.

[2] More detailed descriptions of the Act are to be found in articles by Maher (1981), and McQueary and Risdon (1979).

[3] See Page and Hooper (June, 1982) for a discussion of the various control problems when using computers. Their discussion is enlivened by the imaginative methods used by some employees to line their pockets at the expense of the firm or their colleagues.

[4] See Cooke and Dobing (1984) for a study that proposes general recommendations for the prevention, detection and correction of computer-related errors.

Chapter 4

INTERVIEW RESULTS

This chapter provides the results of the structured interviews with chief executive officers, chief financial officers, internal audit managers and data processing managers. The interviews provided many valuable insights. The results are grouped by topic, with contributions from each management level identified.

DEFINING INTERNAL CONTROL

Chief executive officers (CEOs) and chief financial officers (CFOs) were asked directly about their understanding of the terms "internal control," "management control" and "accounting control". Internal audit managers and data processing managers were asked less directly; their interpretations were revealed through their answers to the interview questions and the ensuing discussions.

In general, the corporate officers interviewed took a broad view of internal control; in their perception, the term embraced accounting, management and operating controls. While definitional differences between corporate positions were small, CEOs took perhaps a slightly broader approach, expressing primary concern for efficiency and productivity. One CEO defined his major internal control concern to be whether the company was spending money legitimately and whether appropriate value was received. Internal control was also defined as including legal and fiduciary aspects such as practices, procedures and safeguarding assets. Avoiding disastrous allocations of capital resources and unwise expenditures were deemed highly relevant.

One manager, who had a fairly representative interpretation, distinguished between a narrow and a broad concept of internal control. He stated that, in the narrow view, internal control referred to financial controls and accounting records, while the broader view was concerned with guarding against inefficiency, waste, and mismanagement of assets, with operating controls constituting an important feature of this concept.

Management Control

Interviewees described management control as part of the administrative function, using internal control policies and procedures described in company manuals designed to secure efficient management and operation of the organization, including efficient use of property and assets to maximize profits. One CEO simply found management control to be synonymous with good management. Long-range planning with appropriate steps for implementation was found to be significant here. Another manager thought that management control was achieved through business plans and objectives, which were monitored through performance review. One CEO described management control as an umbrella term — one that included accounting areas as well as personnel policies and practices.

When pressed, CEOs generally agreed that accounting control was the narrowest concept, but they and several CFOs were a little impatient with the entire idea of distinguishing between the three terms, stating that they were all a part of internal control. None of those interviewed, at any level, distinguished between preventive and detective controls.

Accounting Control

Those who were willing to define accounting control separately perceived it as involving financial controls and accounting records and handled through accounting manuals and procedure bulletins. Frequently included in the definition of accounting control was the idea that it was monitored by an active internal audit.

LEVEL OF CONTROL CONSCIOUSNESS

With respect to internal control, all officers interviewed thought that their companies did a good job. It is interesting that the CEOs expressed greater satisfaction than did the CFOs, whose positions made them more directly responsible for internal control.

The way the high level of control consciousness was explained by the top officer appeared to depend partially on the CEO's personal philosophy and management style. Among the reasons cited were:
- Public emphasis.
- External watchdogs, such as regulatory bodies.
- Frequent internal audits with rigorous follow-ups where results were sent to top management.
- Centralized operations with the CEO being very close to operations and all major decision-making.

Chief financial officers rated their own companies uniformly as having "good" or "very good" internal control. Reasons for the high level of control consciousness included the following:
- Managerial experience.
- Guidance from the parent company.
- Having a highly ethical company.
- Having internal audit monitor deficiencies.
- Being a regulated company (from a utility).
- Decentralization, accompanied by an emphasis on staff integrity.
- Close controls from head office through organizational structure. (This was mentioned often, with divisional controllers or financial vice-presidents being cited as strong features of some companies' internal control environments.)

- Regular meetings and/or debriefing sessions with divisional officers.
- Interest from their audit committee.

The CFOs also identified what they saw as potential areas for improvement. Despite overall confidence, a few stated that some lower-level management in their organizations, such as sales officers, had little idea of internal control. One CEO thought that, in his company, the many engineers in senior management jobs needed to be taught the relationship between internal control, their group controller and internal audit. With these minor exceptions, satisfaction with internal control consciousness was uniformly high.

KEY ELEMENTS OF INTERNAL CONTROL

When each officer was asked what he did himself to strengthen the company's internal control environment, the answers generally fell into categories corresponding with organization theory, such as organization structure, reporting relationships, planning and follow-up. The need to ensure accountability figured prominently in these answers. "Managers do well those things the boss checks" was demonstrated by all CEOs referring to their personal concern and follow-up. Both the audit systems and the actions to correct deficiencies were discussed as being monitored from the top, with one person stating that the findings were used in discussions at individual performance appraisals. In another firm, accountability was primarily handled through budget controls and follow-up.

The CFOs mentioned the primacy of internal audit and follow-up recommendations repeatedly throughout the interviews. As anticipated, CFO activities aimed at strengthening the internal control environment proved to be much more extensive than those of the CEOs. After internal audit, the next major category could be said to fall generally under the heading of organizational structure, rules and policies. The following CFO activities were cited:

- Ensuring the existence of adequate written control policies such as administrative instructions and personnel policies.
- Emphasizing the importance of manuals and bulletins.
- Requiring proper financial authority for appropriations, including subsequent examination of economic conclusions.
- Reviewing a checklist with internal audit.
- Setting standards for project cost control.
- Monitoring of areas such as treasury functions, insurance coverages, and cash management practices.
- Conducting regular meetings with executive vice presidents.

The other major category of officer activity could be broadly termed as performance review. Performance planning with the CFO was also cited. CFOs seemed to think, as did CEOs, that accountability was a major key to the running of their firms, and that interest, concern and follow-up by top officers was a major reason why their internal control was good and their organizations worked well. It was here, also, that it became quite clear that those CFOs found internal control difficult to separate from good management and that, in performing their own managerial activities, the two frequently became indistinguishable.

Additional key elements of internal control were thought to be:
- The attitude of the CFO.
- Having a financial, accounting and auditing sense.
- Having financial-type controls.
- A "management by objectives" program.
- Excellence of management in the field, but with the caveat that financial people in the field with no internal audit checking on them tended to forget about internal control.
- Having a corporate advisory committee for each group, vice president, or division president.
- Training market people and sensitizing them to internal control and developing managers who are extensively involved in the use of company assets.
- Trends in anti-trust and anti-combines legislation.

The interviewees were asked to describe how, in addition to accounting reports, other divisions were monitored. The importance of internal audit was strongly reiterated as a key monitoring device. Additional monitoring techniques included the external auditor's report, financial statistics, production statistics, operation reports, sales and inventory reports, along with regular meetings and regular reports from division heads concerning their divisions' activities.

Non-accounting internal control methods were also mentioned when the interviewees were asked to discuss monitoring techniques. For example, the responses ranged from having key advisory committees, CFOs travelling to the areas in question, tight control of manning levels, attending to customer complaints and even to "stories from neighbouring departments." Having a board selected from different areas of expertise was thought an important aid in internal control, with one company establishing a separate audit committee for joint ventures.

Some officers found that small plants in little communities were an area of vulnerability. They thought that the more isolated operations tended to be less formally run, but that this risk was offset, in large part, by the lower business volume of those plants.

Corporate Codes of Conduct and Company Ethics

All six participating companies had a corporate code of ethics or code of conduct. Listed in increasing order of severity of consequences, breaches of the code of conduct were generally said to result in verbal reprimands, written reprimands, suspensions, and the possibility of dismissal. All stated that their company's tolerance of ethics violations was very low. One CFO referred to "fear" and another summarized his firm's concern by saying that each person should "be able to go on TV and be comfortable with their explanation." All said that, in their experience, very few actions ever needed to be taken.

Executive Perquisites

The question of executive perquisites was approached with interest by the interviewees — nobody displayed the slightest reluctance to discuss the matter. Most admitted that abuse was certainly always possible, but stated that their companies dealt with this matter partly by having relatively few executive perquisites other than company cars and expense accounts that had, in most instances, to pass through internal and external audits. CEO expense accounts were sometimes approved by the CFO — in one instance by a salary committee and, in another instance, only by the CEO himself. The CEO reviewed CFO expense accounts. Club memberships, where applicable, were usually approved at head office.

Some had executive payrolls audited by their external auditor but not by internal audit. Internal audit monitored stock options and those were included in the board of directors' minutes. Not surprisingly, all expressed confidence in their officers' integrity, pointing out that, by the time top corporate office was reached, most companies had had the opportunity for years of observation of each officer.

The issue of "executive override" was stated flatly by one CEO as being not preventable, but, if it occurred, the wrong man had the job. If any employee were faced with a request from a superior that was not legitimate, managers cited the following avenues for disclosure in their companies:
• An ombudsman.
• Employee relations.
• Talk to one's boss's boss, or even to the board.
• A formal grievance procedure.
• Write to the US parent.
• Write to CEO or CFO, with or without anonymity.
• Exit interviews.

One CEO said that investigations would follow to determine whether the occurrence was caused by poor judgment; if the attempt at executive override were more serious, termination could be a result.

INTERNAL CONTROL RISKS

The blurring of definitional lines between internal control, accounting control and management control was highlighted again when CEOs were asked to specify what they thought might be the major internal control risks faced by their companies. One person in the petroleum industry described the possibility of a major lawsuit involving environmental issues, concerning either action or inaction by the company. Another thought that a major risk would be that of a centralized management that failed to fully develop subordinates capable of making decisions.

CFOs also cited general business risks most frequently. Among these were:
• Field plants in small communities.
• Office security (describing a situation where other firms rented space in the headquarters office building).
• Paying too much for goods or services.

- Outside contracts which may be "making them fat".
- Project cost overruns.
- Poor engineering by outside consultants.
- Too much energy and money devoted to regulatory activities (from a utility).
- An objective that cannot be achieved leading to a misstatement of performance. The pressure on the company could be external as well as internal.

More traditional internal control issues were mentioned less frequently, such as:
- Collusion within the company to defraud.
- Pilferage and theft (a retail organization).
- Increased value of the product (petroleum) resulting in more temptation to defraud in the field.

A question concerning specific characteristics of companies that could make internal control particularly easy or difficult illustrated the contingent nature of internal control. A top officer of a regulated firm stated that having only four customers simplified many internal control issues for his company. The topic of risk was investigated further by the questionnaire.

When internal audit managers were asked what they saw as possible major areas of gradual control erosion, responses appeared to be contingent on the companies' environments. They covered a wide range and appeared to be affected by the type of business, organizational structure and geographical locations. They referred to the following possible areas:
- Managers who are responsible for the bottom line and who may cut corners to improve that bottom line.
- External auditors with poor staff who do not understand the role of internal control.
- A retail store where clerks have access to the computer via the cash register and, therefore, to the inventory.
- Purchases made in the field over the allowed spending limit.
- When on-line data processing is instituted (from a company with batch processing).

In their opinion, CFOs found that the 1982-83 recession had affected internal control but assessed this impact to be minor.

THE ROLE OF INTERNAL AUDIT IN INTERNAL CONTROL

While CEOs, and particularly CFOs, thought that the internal audit department unquestionably played a key role in their company's internal control environment, internal audit managers were quick to point out that responsibility for internal control lies with management. Their role was seen as bearing responsibility for appraising, evaluating and monitoring internal control systems already in place and red-flagging weaknesses.

Internal audit managers thought that it was management's decision whether to implement their recommendations — that their role was to make recommendations but not to create controls. In this, they were in complete agreement with those CFOs who thought that it was important for internal audit not to try to second guess management in the field. (It is interesting that the interviewees faulted external audit for this more often than internal audit.)

Internal audit managers saw themselves as consultants and helpers — as a service to be used by management — rather than as police officers. In many instances, internal audit was also used as a training ground for future management personnel.

All internal audit managers described a system of consultation and interaction with their auditees. Auditees were consulted prior to commencement of the audit and, in some cases, could add to the objectives of the audit if they wished. All discussed reports with the auditee upon completion, allowing for disputes with the information (not the recommendation) and changes to the audit report.

Almost all internal audit managers also consulted with the auditee before issuing their audit reports. Some had specific timetables for checking on responses to recommendations. They assessed the timetables to be a strong feature of internal control while others reported their follow-up procedures to be less specific. Of the companies represented in the interviews requiring a written follow-up, some specified a formal time limit such as 60 days or six months. The less specific follow-ups were found to be less satisfactory in these interviewees' opinions.

While most of the internal audit managers did not have anyone who reviewed their actual audit programs, one manager had his audit program reviewed by the treasurer. Several of the companies' CFOs, however, reviewed the audit schedules to ensure that the high-risk areas or special audits could be included in the annual timetable.

None of the internal audit managers had been asked to undertake audit activities by their boards, and virtually all stated that a CEO request would be channeled through their CFO. Special requests generally came from the CFO regarding acquisitions, investigations, shut-down analyses, poor performance investigations, fraud investigations, etc., but these were rare. Most stated that the controller would rarely, if ever, make audit requests, although occasionally a CFO might request special information for meetings.

Questions concerning requests to internal audit from operating managers brought a different response. As mentioned by the interviewees, requests fell into three major categories:

1. Requests concerning areas which the managers thought might be lax in internal control.
2. Requests for internal audit assistance in the construction area for contracts performed on a cost plus basis.
3. Requests to examine computerized systems.

Two of the internal audit managers were concerned about a possible hesitation to request assistance because internal audit reports directly to corporate management. These internal audit managers stated, however, that the company and internal audit would like to see such requests increase.

The proportion of internal audit's resources used for particular activities is given in Table 4.1.

TABLE 4.1

USAGE OF INTERNAL AUDIT RESOURSES
(in percentages)

| | Internal Audit Managers | | | | | |
Resources	Co.1	Co.2	Co.3	Co.4	Co.5	Co.6
Discharge statutory responsibilities (e.g., maintaining accountability to owners)				10		
Profitability and minimization of cost (includes operational efficiency and effectiveness)	60*	35	36	10	45	35
Prevention and detection of fraud and costs		20	1	25	20	20
Safeguarding of assets		35	18	25	20	35
Reliability of accounting records	40*	5	4	20	10	5
Timely preparation of reliable financial information			4		5	
Adherence to other organizational policy		5	1			5
Compliance with external regulations other than GAAP (e.g., FCPA, FIRA, Revenue Canada)			4			
Other: Administration				10		
Cost and benefits of new systems (EDP)			23			
Training			9			
TOTAL	100%	100%	100%	100%	100%	100%

* Listed as 60% of Operations and 40% Financial

Co.1 is a mining company.
Co.2 is a holding company.
Co.3 is a retailing company.
Co.4 is an oil and gas pipeline company.
Co.5 is a petroleum company.
Co.6 is a utility company.

This was further examined by the questionnaire.

All of the internal audit managers gave traditional definitions of the term "asset." Personnel were not considered as assets, but one manager included anything "of financial value to the company including intangibles such as credit account names and addresses" (this was a retailing firm).

Audit schedules were set on an annual basis for the retail organization and varied from a three to four-year schedule in other instances. One interviewee stated that the exposure to risk for vulnerable areas such as payroll, construction and contracts would be a major determination of internal audit activity.

Spending on Internal Control

Budgets for internal audit ranged from a low of $140,000 to a high of $450,000.

When CEOs and CFOs were asked how they would spend an incremental 20 percent on internal control, the basic response was that the current funds allocated were those that could be cost justified. Training in internal control issues and increasing internal control awareness were the major target areas for additional spending, as were the areas of increased internal audit staff, increased frequency of internal audits, performing more operational audits and value-for-money audits. One CFO said that data processing was always a concern and that he would use additional funds to train internal audit staff on new EDP auditing techniques.

All said that they would be reluctant to cut back, but if required would:

1. Reduce internal audit staff, which would require reducing frequency of internal audits, forcing greater selectivity.
2. Eliminate some reports. One would eliminate quarterly budget variance reports — he stated that they "rarely turned up important things."

Internal audit managers thought that they would like more capability to audit EDP operations, with some being interested in performing more operational audits.

Organization of Internal Audit

As anticipated, internal audit was centralized in the companies interviewed. One, however, reported a subsidiary that had its own internal audit, and a retail company reported that some cash-audit operations — an obviously sensitive area — were carried out by an operating or office manager. That appeared to be supplementary to the regular internal audit. Internal audit reported to the parent company if the parent was located elsewhere.

Reporting was basically to the chief financial officer, and to the audit committee — a structure that ensured that internal audit was independent of its auditees. Most discussed each audit report with their CFO before issuing it, with the report also going to the department audited and the audit committee. Depending on the structure of the company, some also sent each audit report to the company controller and their parent. A few also sent the audit reports to their external auditors.

Relationship with External Audit

Most internal audit managers indicated that their external auditors reviewed their internal audit programs as part of the external audit. One internal audit department performed all the data processing activities for external audit, another confirmed all receivables because of its time-consuming nature, some did cash audits, some did inventory counts and another did payroll.

Doing some work in coordination with external audit was cited by four of the interviewees. Overall, the work of internal audit could be described as time saving for the company on external audit. Most internal auditors did not think that more than 15 to 20 percent of external audit fees were saved by their activities. The researchers' distinct perception was that internal auditors perceived their work to be concerned with far more than financial statement matters.

Most internal audit managers saw no change in their relationship with their external auditors as company systems underwent changes from manual to electronic data processing. One manager, however, foresaw external audit in the future relying extensively on internal audit's reviews of EDP systems due to the difficulty of securing sufficient expertise by external audit, the time-consuming nature of these audits and the familiarity of an internal audit department with its own systems.

A different perspective was expressed by data processing managers, however, who discussed the problem of internal audit managers being cautious about data processing activities. A few reported their internal audit departments to have very capable EDP auditors, but others found that internal audit lacked real EDP expertise and did not understand the EDP operations sufficiently. When internal audit managers were asked to speculate about the future, however, the major change predicted in internal audit was that of increased emphasis on data processing.

Other future changes also hinged around data processing. A preference for computer science degree qualification for data processing auditors was expressed by several managers. A number of others forecast that operational auditing would play a larger role in the future.

For improvement in internal control, internal audit managers had a narrower range of prescriptions. Suggested were:

- Training of personnel to improve awareness of internal control.
- Paper flow improvement.
- More consultation with internal audit concerning data processing.

A continual personnel rotation in internal audit was seen as a problem because internal audit was, for some companies, a training ground for managers.

If the perceptions of most of the internal audit managers are correct, the contribution of internal audit to their organizations is considerable. Most internal audit managers thought that, in the past year, they had made significant contributions to internal control and the organization. One said that his department was responsible for identifying an incompetent financial officer, thus turning a division around. Others also cited identification of poor managers. Finding and correcting poor management of projects was another example and of contractors yet another. Several thought that their contributions had saved their companies a great deal of money.

THE AUDIT COMMITTEE

Each CEO reported that his audit committee was composed entirely of outside board members. This issue was further explored by questionnaire. Each company had both internal audit and external audit reporting on internal control to the audit committee. CFOs and internal audit managers described their audit committee as being concerned with internal control, but not generally reviewing it in depth (also, see CICA, 1981).

INTERNAL CONTROL AND DATA PROCESSING

A great deal of concern has been expressed in the literature about developments in data processing that have complicated internal control. This has been brought ·about by rapidly advancing technology as well as the increased use of computers for data storage, recordkeeping, preparation of financial statements, forecasting and other operational activities. Recognizing this, the interview guide for data processing managers was designed to secure information about the nature of the systems in place as well as about internal control. For example, whether particular systems may give rise to particular internal control problems is a relevant question when considering internal control environments. Another current issue is whether personnel expertise has kept pace sufficiently with computer hardware and software technology.

Questions asked data processing managers centred around three areas:
1. The firm's computer environment — how data processing fits into the organization, and what managers perceived the role of data processing in their company to be.
2. Internal control aspects of their company's electronic data processing activities. This included their perception of internal control risks.
3. Internal audit involvement with data processing systems.

Data Processing in the Organization

Data processing managers viewed their function as a staff function — one that provides a service to the organization. Generally, they thought that responsibility for internal control in EDP systems was, of necessity, a shared responsibility and included:
- Users of the system being responsible for specifying policies and procedures.
- Data processing manager ensuring that policies are followed.
- Internal and external audit being responsible for maintaining internal control over data processing.

The idea was explored that, historically, data processing users would likely have been held primarily responsible for internal control.

Some data processing centres were profit centres with a "fee for service" basis of chargeback. Some had centralized data processing, others were decentralized. Some had on-line realtime update, but batch processing still existed. Use of data processing services was divided about equally in these corporations between accounting, finance activities and operational activities. This aspect was explored further on the questionnaires.

Most data processing managers interviewed reported to the vice president of finance or chief financial officer, but one manager of a decentralized operation reported to the general manager of administration in his provincial group.

When managers were asked to discuss changes in data processing that had taken place, several trends were identified. One was a shift in usage patterns, with distribution sites using computers more. Along the same line, changes from supporting mostly accounting functions to supporting more operations and staff departments were cited. Growth of 35 percent per year for the past five years was reported by one firm. Increased usage for communications and clerical level work was very widespread but not thought to affect internal control significantly.

Although terminals were common in the firms interviewed, microcomputers had not had a major impact on internal control. Some referred to the presence of a few microcomputers that interacted with the mainframe, but this was not widespread. Some companies had desktop computers, but the general impression was one of caution, a wait-and-see attitude. Some expressed concerns about standardization and noted that their firms had not yet developed any guidelines or policies on microcomputers. Some foresaw increased future use of micros by administration for fiscal planning and graphics. They did not appear to think, however, that such increased use of microcomputers would present any significant internal control problems.

Concerning the organization of data processing, one question dealt with the level of control exercised by corporate data processing over divisional data processing. One corporation had a completely centralized system, with corporate data processing in charge of decision making about operations and systems; another allowed for divisional representation. One manager reported that his firm relied on a system of "Seven Ps" which were rules documented in writing:

1. Written policies, including internal control.
2. Procedures concerning the acquisition of equipment.
3. Priorities (set in executive meetings).
4. Plan around the priorities.
5. Personnel — particularly the tracking of who is available.
6. Production — meaning the ability to produce.
7. Performance review.

To illustrate the variety in the practice of organizational control over data processing, another data processing manager expressed frustration about the failure of his firm to specify the mission of data processing. He stated that, while data processing groups throughout the company were free to do what they wanted, most did not really like that. He found data processing in his firm to be in a state of flux and thought that, while most other managers did not really want to be bothered with data processing expertise, it would be helpful to have a diverse group within the firm address the broader issues, prepare a position paper and issue some guidelines for computer policy.

Data processing is a considerable expense to corporations. Budgets ranged from a high of $10 million to a low of $1.7 million. For most, personnel costs were greater than hardware costs (see Table 4.2). Of interest is the relative spending between personnel versus hardware. Most would have liked more resources — some citing backlogs or the usual "wishes" that administrative groups everywhere have. The majority would spend most of a hypothetical budget increase on personnel first.

TABLE 4.2

DATA PROCESSING ANNUAL BUDGET (000's)

	Co.1	Co.2	Co.3.	Co.4	Co.5
Annual budget	$6,000	$8,000	$10,000	$1,700	$2,000
Approximate distribution among:					
Personnel	3,000	4,000	2,200	850	1,000
Hardware (purchase, rental,					
maintenance)	2,400	2,400	6,500	680	500
All other	600	1,600	1,300	170	500

Co.1 is a mining company.
Co.2 is a holding company.
Co.3 is a retailing company.
Co.4 is an oil and gas pipeline company.
Co.5 is a petroleum company.

When asked about their use of outside data processing services and whether any potentially sensitive programs or data were made available to the outside supplier, most reported little use of outside services for sensitive data, except for one whose business plans were in a time-shared modelling service and another whose subsidiaries used payroll services from banks. In addition, use of outside data processing services were reported generally as a supplement to internal facilities or expertise such as:
• Programming in a minor way.
• Statistical services.
• On a consulting basis such as for "renting" supplemental development people.
• Specialized time-sharing services.
• Use of local commercial bureaus by a few subsidiaries.

To safeguard the time-shared data, one organization supplied only coded information, but most relied on controls such as passwords.

Data sharing between application areas was found in all but one of the companies interviewed, with concurrent sharing where the system allowed it. Multiple uses of single applications were found, with trends toward reduction of existing batch systems and realtime update.

Features of EDP Control Systems

Physical control over computer hardware was accomplished in the selected companies through locks and closely restricted access. Password clearance was used to control access to terminals, together with protective phone numbers, pre-clearance of access to the system wanted and, sometimes, secondary and tertiary passwords. Certain terminals were not given access to certain transactions and programs. One company, which sent computerized data a long distance to head office, expressed some concern about use of microwave transmission that could be monitored by satellite.

Use of the computer system itself was generally controlled through user IDs and passwords. Use of specific programs was handled by codes for each system with certain users being allowed to sign on only to given applications. Some stated that, for the opening of a specific data file, a person having application access would usually have access to the data in that file. For access to specific data fields in a file, specific records in a file or specific data fields in a specific record, most used only the above controls. Doubts were frankly expressed, however, about control of computer access by some data processing managers who believed that their systems' passwords and codes were normally adequate, but that a smart analyst could probably "screw up the system." Another said he and his organization were "fledglings in this area."

Control over program changes was a well-defined process for the participant corporations. Most followed a system similar to the one described below:

1. An authorized person, usually the user who initiated the process, makes a written change request.
2. A different authorized person signs off the proposed changes.
3. The change is made on the source program.
4. A copy of the program is tested and then the whole system is tested on those copies.
5. The user okays the changes made and signs approval.
6. The computer operations supervisor receives the new program and signs approval.
7. The program goes from the development library to the production library.

Thus, changes were reviewed by both operations and data processing people.

Data processing managers interviewed expressed some concerns about the security of their systems. Some examples of weaknesses they mentioned were:
• Physical access to computer facilities.
• Run-to-run balancing in older systems.
• Access to data.
• Speed of technical change resulting in precautions no longer being adequate.
• Telecommunications where information was transmitted by telephone.

Those concerns were explored further by the questionnaire.

Respondents were also asked whether it would be possible for someone in a position of trust to:

(a) Sabotage equipment.
(b) Remove the accounts receivable file.

(c) Remove a copy of customer files.
(d) Read sensitive information from the personnel file (salaries).
(e) Modify the accounts payable file.
(f) Modify the accounts receivable program.

The responses are outlined in Table 4.3

TABLE 4.3

**NUMBER OF FIRMS* RESPONDING AFFIRMATIVELY
CONCERNING COMPUTER CONTROL WEAKNESSES**

Position	Possible Action					
	a	b	c	d	e	f
Senior Analyst	4	3	3	2	4	3
Junior Programmer	3	2	2	1	2	1
Manufacturers' Customer Engineer	5	0	0	1	1	0
Internal Auditor	2	1	1	2	0	0
External Auditor	2	1	1	1	0	0
A Visiting Consultant	2	0	0	2	1	0

*Five firms were asked this question.

Backup and recovery plans appeared to present little problem in these particular systems because backup copies were made as frequently as data files were updated. Backup storage was always at a separate site — one in the same building, but others more distant, with two at underground locations. Transaction files were maintained on average for about a year, except where regulatory requirements dictated a longer period. Data loss was reported as being either nonexistent or minimal with recovery time varying between one or a few hours, depending on the nature of the loss.

Backup and recovery plans for the computer facilities, however, were less rigorous. All the firms had backup plans but only two had tested them. Backup facilities were all external to the company but had been reviewed by the external auditor. In one instance, the backup plan had been formulated in response to an external auditor's recommendation.

As for their own responsibility in control of data processing, managers thought that guarding against data loss was very important, followed closely by controlling data access. Maintaining data quality was generally perceived to be the overall responsibility of the user. Senior analysts were generally responsible for the design of the system, which was assessed by some to be the most important responsibility of all.

When asked which data processing systems were particularly sensitive, possibly because of potentially large misuse of corporate resources should control be lacking, the responses appeared to be somewhat contingent upon the industry.

Most referred to accounting systems with payroll, accounts payable and accounts receivable also seen as sensitive areas, as was inventory. More data on risk assessment was collected by the questionnaire.

The Role of Internal Auditor in Control of Data Processing

Both internal audit and data processing managers were asked about the history of the involvement of internal audit in the development and operation of EDP systems. Company practice varied a great deal, ranging from close involvement in a firm where the internal audit manager was once head of data processing to no involvement at all. One internal audit manager described involvement as "a struggle." Two reported that internal auditors were active members of their EDP steering committees. Most thought that such involvement was either increasing or likely to increase. Everyone supported close ties between the two departments on development.

Three companies used a formal methodology for controlling the design and implementation of EDP systems — another company had developed its own methodology described by its manager as less formal.

Six phases were described for an implementation system. Generally, they were as follows:

1. Systems definition of requirements — the users tell you what they want.
2. Specify alternatives and select one.
3. External specifications stage — major systems are defined.
4. Programming and design.
5. Implementation.
6. Post mortem.

A data processing manager, whose firm had no procedure, expressed the need for a formal method. Another manager declared that his users "want to know, without spending any money, what it would cost for an 'unspecified' system."

While users are heavily involved, particularly in the first and second phases, internal audit may be involved in an advisory capacity, but not always in sign-off. One manager found that his users liked to have data processing assist on internal control. Internal audit managers saw their involvement as being somewhat more significant than data processing managers did. They reported little involvement in operations, particularly with engineering systems and modelling systems. Those were not reviewed by internal audit, presumably because they present little internal control risk.

Internal auditors stated that when they were involved, they ensured that audit trails were present and controls were built in. Applications were reviewed during internal audits. Data processing managers did not perceive internal audit in these companies as being specifically concerned with changes in programs once they were operational, but stated that internal audit would check all systems' changes requests if and when the total system were audited. This area was also explored further by the questionnaires.

When asked whether internal audit had sufficient expertise in data processing, all data processing managers thought there was adequate expertise, but they would appreciate more internal audit staff who were specifically EDP trained. EDP auditors came from a variety of sources — some from within the company. A potential problem was seen concerning the career path of such a person, particularly a lack of advancement opportunity.

None of the data processing managers thought that pressure to get a system up quickly resulted in a reduction of internal controls built into the system, although a minor concern was expressed that the testing phase of a new system could possibly be shortened. One stated that a few crash, one-time efforts, such as special reports had been required that, typically, were government-induced (from a regulated industry).

External Audit of Data Processing Operations

The role of the external auditor in the audit of data processing was explored. External auditors audited, as expected, once a year, checking for accuracy and documentation of the systems. Data processing managers were generally less impressed with external audit than with their own internal auditors, using phrases such as "they audit around the computer, since few are able to audit with the computer." One company's external auditor, it was said, never audited data processing systems. Another manager stated that his department had, on three occasions, specifically asked for a special audit but that these had not been very satisfactory. Such concerns are also well represented in the literature (Mautz, Merten and Severance, 1983, pp. 52-53).

Finally, data processing managers discussed whether they thought their personnel were trained in and motivated by internal control considerations. Their regard for their staff's concern and knowledge of internal control was quite high. The entire topic was of great interest to these managers and, despite differing backgrounds, there was common accord about the importance of internal control in the operation of their area.

US FOREIGN CORRUPT PRACTICES ACT

Canadian corporations with US parents were affected by the requirements of the US Foreign Corrupt Practices Act, which requires companies to maintain adequate books and records and to devise and maintain adequate internal control systems.

They stated that, in their opinion, having to comply with the act's provisions had been helpful internally, because their company had performed a major inquiry and had examined internal control very closely. Documentation such as operating manuals, policy manuals, financial authority manuals and bulletins describing operating procedures in an office environment were listed as being positive outcomes of the internal control examination. Others said that they submit a quarterly report to their US parent, but it made little difference because their controls were already good. One internal audit manager stated that, at the time the requirements of the FCPA were implemented, the company's internal audit staff grew significantly.

Chapter 5

QUESTIONNAIRE RESULTS PART I: SUMMARY BY MANAGERIAL LEVEL

This chapter presents the responses of chief financial officers, internal audit managers and data processing managers to the questionnaires. Some questions were asked of all three groups, but many questions were group specific. This chapter presents the responses of each managerial group separately and Chapter 6 presents cross-group and cross-country comparisons.

The statistical techniques of one-way and two-way analyses of variance were used in this chapter to measure the level of significance found by comparing responses associated with industry groupings and company size groupings. If an analysis of variance identifies differences as being significant at the .05 level, for example, it means that there is only a five percent chance that the difference in responses by groups is a random variation. In this study, only those differences proving to be statistically significant at the .05 level or less are reported.[1]

This chapter is divided into four sections: the first presents a profile of the three managerial groups and of characteristics of the internal audit and data processing departments; the following three sections present the responses of each of the managerial groups surveyed.

PROFILE OF RESPONDENTS AND THE CHARACTERISTICS OF THE INTERNAL AUDIT AND DATA PROCESSING DEPARTMENTS

This section presents data collected from demographic questions asked of the chief financial officers, data processing managers and internal audit managers. Characteristics of the internal audit and data processing departments are then described. For data presented in percentage form, some response totals exceed 100 percent because multiple answers were given to a single question; and a few total less than 100 percent because of omitted responses.

As indicated in Table 5.1, more than 90 percent of the responding chief financial officers, internal audit managers and data processing managers were male.

TABLE 5.1

MANAGERIAL GROUP BY SEX

	Male (%)	Female (%)
Chief financial officers	97.7	2.3
Internal audit managers	90.7	9.3
Data processing managers	95.3	4.7

Table 5.2 details university degrees held by the three managerial levels. The most frequently cited degrees held by chief financial officers and internal audit managers were in business or the arts. The most common university degrees held by data processing managers were bachelor's degrees in engineering, mathematics or science. Overall, fewer data processing managers held degrees.

TABLE 5.2

UNIVERSITY DEGREES HELD BY MANAGERIAL GROUP

	Chief Financial Officer (%)	Internal Audit Manager (%)	Data Processing Manager (%)
Officers holding degrees	74.5	70.0	59.1
Types of Degrees Held:			
Bachelor's degree in commerce or business	56.1	59.1	13.8
Bachelor's degree in arts	18.7	20.4	13.8
Bachelor's degree in science engineering or mathematics	9.4	8.0	43.0
Master's degree in business administration	7.6	4.4	12.2
Master's degree in arts	2.3	0.7	1.6
Master's degree in science	0.0	2.2	5.7
Law degree	0.6	0.7	0.8
Other degrees	5.3	0.8	9.1

As indicated in Table 5.3, chief financial officers and internal audit managers were found more likely to have professional designations than data processing managers.

TABLE 5.3

MANAGERIAL GROUP BY RESPONDENTS WITH PROFESSIONAL DESIGNATIONS

Managerial Group	Professional Designations — All Respondents (%)	Designations Held By Respondents Without University Degrees (%)
Chief financial officer	81.7	91.9
Internal audit manager	84.1	77.3
Data processing manager	36.1	30.9

Professional designations held by respondents are presented in Table 5.4. The most common were accounting designations. Data processing managers held a wider variety of designations outside the accounting field, as would be expected, including professional engineering (17.3 percent) and certified data processing (14.8 percent) credentials.

TABLE 5.4

PROFESSIONAL ACCOUNTING DESIGNATION BY MANAGERIAL GROUP

	Managerial Group		
Professional Designations	**Chief Financial Officer (%)**	**Internal Audit Manager (%)**	**Data Processing Manager (%)**
Chartered Accountant	74.1	60.9	13.3
Registered Industrial Accountant	13.0	18.7	18.5
Certified General Accountant	5.3	7.7	4.9

The respondents were asked to classify their firms by size. The results are presented in Table 5.5. Slightly more data processing managers characterized their firms as small and medium than did chief financial officers or internal audit managers.

TABLE 5.5

MANAGERIAL GROUP BY SELF-CATEGORIZED FIRM SIZE

	Firm Size		
Managerial Group	**Small (%)**	**Medium (%)**	**Large (%)**
Chief financial officer	5.8	28.6	65.6
Internal audit manager	4.4	35.5	60.1
Data processing manager	7.5	44.2	48.3

The three managerial groups were asked to indicate whether they were employed in government regulated companies. The responding chief financial officers reported being employed less frequently by regulated firms than were the other two managerial groups. The percentage of managerial groups employed by regulated companies was:

Chief financial officer	33.5%
Internal audit manager	47.5%
Data processing manager	45.0%

Table 5.6 presents statistics about internal audit and data processing managers. The average age of those two management groups was approximately the same, but data processing managers were found to remain with the same firm and in the same department longer than did internal audit managers. This evidence suggests that data processing managers spent more time attaining their current position than did their internal audit counterparts.

TABLE 5.6

EMPLOYMENT DATA IN YEARS BY MANAGERIAL GROUP

	Managerial Group	
	Internal Audit (years)	Data Processing (years)
Employed by same firm:		
Mean number of years	9	11.3
Median number of years	6	8.4
Employed in present department:		
Mean number of years	6	15.5
Range of years	1 to 26	1 to 34
Held present management position:		
Mean number of years	(Not asked)	5.3
Average age range	35 to 45	35 to 45

Because many new internal audit staff have already been selected as financial management recruits and have been placed in internal audit partially for training purposes, this would also help to explain why data processing managers, who probably were not originally designated as management trainees, spend longer on average in their departments.

Composition of Internal Audit Department

When asked to describe their internal audit departments, the responses of chief financial officers and internal audit managers differed, as shown in Table 5.7.

TABLE 5.7

**DESCRIPTION OF INTERNAL AUDIT DEPARTMENT
BY MANAGERIAL GROUP**

	Managerial Group	
	Chief Financial Officer	Internal Audit Manager
Mean number of staff members	10.94	9.38
Median number of staff members	4.89	4.37
Range of staff size	1 to 99	1 to 99

The general characteristics of internal audit staff were addressed on the internal audit manager questionnaire.

Firms with internal audit used as an entry-level department for new financial management recruits	51.8%
Average number of years new recruits remained in internal audit	2.8

Specific questions were asked about the computer audit specialist. Internal audit managers stated that:

An individual was designated as a computer audit specialist	47.1%
The average number of years spent in internal audit by computer audit specialists was	4.2
The specialist was likely to be hired internally	48.1%
The specialist was hired from the EDP or information systems area	67.2%

Table 5.8 indicates university degrees held by internal audit recruits. The most common degrees held were in business and computing science, with other degrees including bachelors' degrees in arts, science and engineering.

A computer audit specialist was less likely to possess a university degree, but, of the degrees held, a bachelor's degree in computing science ranked first, closely followed by a bachelor's degree in business.

TABLE 5.8

UNIVERSITY DEGREE HELD BY INTERNAL AUDIT RECRUITS

	Recruiting Category	
Degree Held	All Recruits (%)	Computer Audit Specialists (%)
Bachelor's degree in business or commerce	68.5	24.6
Bachelor's degree in computing science	12.9	26.7
All other degrees	22.0	6.0

Table 5.9 reports on professional designations. The average new recruit possessed an accounting designation or was a student in an accounting program. The three most common credentials were chartered accountant, registered industrial accountant and the certified general accountant. Other designations held by internal audit recruits were those of certified internal auditor, and certified public accountant.

As shown in Table 5.9, a computer audit specialist was less likely to hold a professional accounting designation than other internal audit recruits.

TABLE 5.9

PROFESSIONAL DESIGNATIONS HELD BY TYPE OF INTERNAL AUDIT RECRUITS

	Recruiting Category	
Professional Designation	All Recruits (%)	Computer Audit Specialists (%)
Chartered Accountant	55.6	19.4
Registered Industrial Accountant	48.3	12.5
Certified General Accountant	34.5	7.3

Data processing managers also provided information about the systems audit specialist. They reported the following in their companies:

An internal audit team member was designated as a computerized information systems audit specialist	47.2%
Data processing specialists were rotated into internal audit to act as technical consultants	90.7%
Average number of years data processing specialists spent in internal audit	3.0
Range of years spent in internal audit by data processing specialists	1 to 10

A one-way analysis of variance found a statistically significant difference at the .0001 level between size of firm and the presence of a computerized information systems audit specialist. As expected, an audit specialist was more often employed in large firms than in small or medium-sized firms.

Composition of Data Processing Staff

Two questions yielded information on the personnel within the data processing managers' departments. The percentage of new recruits to the data processing area holding a university degree (some held more than one degree) was:

Computing science degree	69.4%
Business degree	34.0%
All other degrees	15.7%

New data processing recruits did not have professional credentials as often as did internal audit recruits. Only 6 percent of new recruits held professional certificates, but certificates and diplomas from trade schools or community colleges were held by data processing recruits more often than by recruits to the internal audit area (39.7 percent as compared to 2.1 percent). This reflects the differing expertise of the two functional areas.

The percentage of staff hired internally by the data processing department was 65.5 percent. Of those hired internally, their preceding department was:

Accounting	23.6%
Finance	7.6%
Operations	3.2%

The remaining 65.6 percent were hired from all other areas including retailing, manufacturing, internal audit and planning.

CHIEF FINANCIAL OFFICER RESPONSES

The following section presents data gathered from the chief financial officers' questionnaires.

Communication of Internal Control Policies

Chief financial officers were asked how their companies communicated internal control measures and practices to employees. They reported acknowledgement of the existence of a control system by reference to it in policy letters, management statements, delegation of authority and job description as:

Extensive	56.8%
To some extent	42.1%
Not at all	1.2%

Table 5.10 reports whether a comprehensive effort was made to convey internal control practices to specific groups of employees. CFOs thought the majority of company staff was informed about objectives, personal responsibilities and applicable internal control measures. As expected, company officers and key employees were provided with more information than other employees were.

TABLE 5.10

COMMUNICATION OF INTERNAL CONTROL INFORMATION BY EMPLOYEE CATEGORY
(CFO Response)

	Employee Category	
	Officers and Key Employees	Others
Information	(%)	(%)
Company objectives	92.0	59.7
Their personal responsibilities	90.9	83.7
Applicable internal control measures	82.1	69.6

Almost 50 percent of chief financial officers characterized their firms' company manuals as providing a complete or almost complete description of internal control. Degree of coverage was described as:

Complete	9.5%
Almost complete	39.3%
Partial	37.8%
Very little	12.6%

Corporate Codes of Conduct

Companies having written codes of conduct constituted 63.5 percent of the sample. Company size was not statistically significant for this practice. Codes of conduct were, however, reported as existing in regulated companies significantly more often than in nonregulated companies (.05 level).

For companies with codes of conduct, a majority of officers and other employees received copies. Table 5.11 shows that although a majority of officers and key employees signed for conformity with the corporate code of conduct, other employees signed less frequently (Table 5.11).

TABLE 5.11

CODE OF CONDUCT PRACTICES BY EMPLOYEE CATEGORY
(CFO Response)

	Employee Category	
	Officers and Key Employees	Others
Practices	(%)	(%)
Codes of conduct received by	97.1	59.3
Periodically signed for conformity with the code by	71.3	20.3

The percentage of companies having disciplinary procedures for violations of the code of conduct was 65.0 percent. The firm's size did not affect whether a company had disciplinary procedures. Of those having disciplinary measures, 72.4 percent had had cause to enforce them. A one-way analysis of variance identified significant differences by company size (.01 level), with larger companies enforcing disciplinary procedures more frequently.

The percentage of companies that had a designated person to whom an employee could report bypassing of company policy on internal control was 43.7 percent. Statistically significant differences (.04 level) by size were identified, with smaller companies having a designated person less often.

The most frequently mentioned "Other" way of discovering a bypass of company policy or internal controls was internal audit (10 percent). Mentioned less frequently was external audit (1.8 percent), followed by observations made by customers (1.5 percent).

Objectives of Internal Control

Table 5.12 provides data on the importance of certain internal control objectives within the firm. On average, CFOs ranked the objectives of internal control in the following order:

1. Safeguarding of assets.
2. Ensuring reliability of accounting records.
3. Prevention and detection of error.
4. Prevention and detection of fraud.
5. Ensuring orderly and efficient conduct of business.
6. Ensuring compliance with management policies.
7. Profitability and minimization of costs.
8. Assuring effective use of company resources.
9. Discharging statutory responsibility to owners.
10. Timely preparation of financial statements.

TABLE 5.12

CFO PERCEPTION OF INTERNAL CONTROL OBJECTIVES BY DEGREE OF IMPORTANCE

	Degree of Importance			
Objectives	Very Important (%)	Somewhat Important (%)	Of Little Importance (%)	Not Important (%)
Prevention and detection of fraud	73.2	24.5	1.9	0.4
Prevention and detection of error	79.2	20.0	0.8	0.0
Ensuring orderly and efficient conduct of business	68.2	28.3	3.1	0.4
Discharging statutory responsibilities to owners	47.5	38.5	11.7	2.3
Safeguarding of assets	85.3	12.7	1.9	0.0
Profitability and minimization of costs	55.2	32.8	11.2	0.8
Assuring effective use of company resources	52.5	34.4	12.4	0.8
Ensuring reliability of accounting records	83.5	14.6	1.9	0.0
Timely preparation of financial statements	46.4	36.8	13.0	3.8
Ensuring compliance with management policies	69.1	25.9	4.6	0.4

Responsibility for Internal Control Systems

Companies clearly stating responsibility of different positions and levels of authority in company manuals or instructions constituted 66.5 percent of the sample.

Responsibility for Reporting

Table 5.13 indicates the organizational level(s) where various responsibilities for internal control systems were concentrated, as described by the CFO. The controller was reported to have primary responsibility for design of internal control systems. The CFO reported having responsibility for approval of the system, together with others such as the CEO and the board or audit committee. Responsibility for the evaluation of system effectiveness was assigned primarily to external and internal auditors. The CFO, controller and CEO were the major participants in authorizing changes to the system. It should be noted that there was considerable overlap in assignment of responsibility to the various levels.

TABLE 5.13

MANAGERIAL LEVEL BY SYSTEMS RESPONSIBILITY
(CFO Response)

	Responsibility			
Managerial Level	**Designs Internal Control System (%)**	**Approves the System (%)**	**Evaluates Systems Effectiveness (%)**	**Authorizes Changes to the System (%)**
Chief financial officer	14.6	83.3	27.9	67.0
Controller or chief accounting officer	78.5	35.5	32.6	45.9
Internal audit manager	27.4	16.4	89.1	8.0
Chief executive officer	1.9	62.1	21.4	51.5
External auditor	5.5	4.5	97.5	1.0
Audit committee or board	1.9	31.1	69.8	19.8

Managerial reporting responsibilities are also shown in Table 5.14. CFOs stated that the internal audit manager was responsible for reporting on internal control to both financial and senior management. The CEO was designated most often as having responsibility for reporting on internal control to the board or audit committee. The data processing manager's report was most frequently received by the CFO.

TABLE 5.14

MANAGERIAL REPORTING RESPONSIBILITIES
(CFO Response)

	Responsibility			
Managerial Level	**Reports on Internal Control to Financial Management (%)**	**Reports on Internal Control to Senior Management (%)**	**Reports on Internal Control to Board or Audit Committee (%)**	**Receives Data Processing Manager's Report (%)**
Chief executive officer	19.1	33.6	77.1	27.5
Chief financial officer	29.2	57.1	66.8	52.7
Controller	67.7	52.8	20.5	35.4
Internal audit	73.6	66.5	53.3	19.8
External audit	60.1	54.7	71.9	11.8
Line manager	51.5	36.6	4.0	35.6

Budgeting

Table 5.15 provides data on the organizational levels at which various budgeting activities occurred. All organizational levels were involved in budgeting, but corporate management was the only level overwhelmingly involved in all budgeting aspects.

TABLE 5.15

BUDGETING ACTIVITIES BY ORGANIZATIONAL LEVEL
(CFO Response)

	Organizational Level			
	---	---	---	---
Budget Activity	**Unit or Department Management (%)**	**Divisional Management (%)**	**Corporate Management (%)**	**Board of Directors (%)**
Participation in the budget setting process	89.6	85.3	82.2	13.9
Reviews the master budget	8.8	44.6	94.2	65.0
Compares actual results with budgeted results	64.6	80.4	92.3	58.5
Reviews explanations of documented material differences	36.6	70.8	91.4	49.4

CFOs indicated the extent to which certain types of expenditures were controlled and the level of approval required to exceed those limits. These are shown in Table 5.16. Results indicate that a majority of firms had either budgeted amounts or fixed maximum amounts which, if exceeded, required the approval of a senior officer, senior management or the full board.

TABLE 5.16

EXPENDITURE CATEGORY BY EXTENT OF BUDGETING CONTROLS
AND APPROVAL LEVEL
(CFO Response)

	Nature of Limit			
	---	---	---	---
Expenditure Category	**None (%)**	**Budgeted Amount (%)**	**Fixed Maximum Amount (%)**	**Level of Approval Required to Exceed Limit**
Operating expenditures	19.9	64.3	15.8	Senior officer
Inventory purchases	41.3	38.6	20.2	Senior officer
Capital expenditures	1.3	54.1	44.6	Full board
Incurrence of debt:				
Under one year	30.3	26.5	43.1	Full board or senior management
More than one year	20.4	27.0	52.6	Full board
Contracts to sell or provide a service	44.1	26.1	29.9	Senior management

Cost-Benefit Analyses of Internal Control Systems Change
The following types of cost-benefit analyses were described as having been undertaken before significant changes were introduced to the internal control system:

Formal analysis	22.2%
Informal analysis	65.0%
No analysis	12.8%

Compliance Monitoring of Internal Control
Companies providing for a monitoring of their internal control procedures were 84.8 percent. The percentage of CFOs who assessed their compliance monitoring as excessive, about right or less than desirable was as follows:

Excessive	0.8%
About right	76.4%
Less than desirable	14.4%

Companies' compliance monitoring was provided by:

Internal audit function	73.1%
Controller's department	68.4%
Systems specialist	17.9%
External auditors	74.9%
Others	4.5%

"Others" in this question included the chief financial officer, line management reviews, financial reviews and outside consultants. Almost all respondents reported the involvement of several organizational levels in compliance monitoring, indicating the importance of monitoring activities.

Suggestions for Internal Control Improvements
Those responsible for the last major internal control improvement were:

	Number of firms
Internal audit	35
Controller	25
Chief financial officer	20
External audit	5
Parent company	3

Also cited, but infrequently, were chief executive officer, department manager, accounting department and senior vice presidents. It should be noted that most of the suggestions made for major internal control improvements were internally generated.

Rating of Systems

Table 5.17 presents data on a self-assessment of respondents' firms' internal control systems, internal audit systems and internal audit of their computerized systems. Internal control systems were rated as excellent or approaching excellence by 38 percent of chief financial officers. For internal audit systems, 36.2 percent of chief financial officers ranked their systems as excellent or approaching excellence. For internal audit of computerized systems, 18.5 percent of chief financial officers ranked their companies as excellent or approaching excellence.

TABLE 5.17

CFO ASSESSMENT OF INTERNAL CONTROL BY SYSTEM

	System		
Rating	Internal Control System (%)	Internal Audit System (%)	Internal Audit of Computerized System (%)
Excellent — includes all measures that can be justified	18.2	13.3	4.5
Approaching excellence — final improvements are either in process of implementation or under consideration	19.8	22.9	14.0
Satisfactory — needs minor improvement	58.5	44.2	52.5
Needs major improvement	3.1	14.6	26.0

Consistency of Internal Control

Of the respondents, 59.6 percent reported inconsistent quality of internal control throughout the company. Table 5.18 ranks reasons for inconsistency of internal control within the respondents' companies. Overall, the three most important reasons for lack of consistency, in descending order, were:

1. Characteristics of a specific division or unit.
2. Characteristics of a division or unit's staff.
3. Lack of management attention.

Other reasons given in addition to those in Table 5.18 included government intervention and lack of manuals.

TABLE 5.18

**REASONS FOR INTERNAL CONTROL INCONSISTENCIES
RANKED BY IMPORTANCE
(CFO Response)**

	Degree of Importance				
Reasons	**Most Important (%)**	**Second (%)**	**Third (%)**	**Fourth (%)**	**Least Important (%)**
Lack of management attention	13.7	4.9	5.3	3.0	4.6
Characteristics of parent company	2.3	1.5	3.0	1.5	2.3
Changes in key personnel	3.0	3.8	2.7	1.9	2.3
General personnel turnover	1.5	3.0	3.0	3.0	1.9
Differing standards of appropriate conduct arising from dissimilar cultural backgrounds	1.1	1.1	3.4	4.6	1.1
Geographic dispersion	5.7	3.8	5.3	5.3	4.6
Recent business acquisitions	3.8	4.2	1.5	1.9	1.1
Characteristics of a specific division or unit, for example maturity, nature of activity or business, organizational structure	10.3	11.0	5.3	3.4	1.1
Characteristics of the division or unit staff, for example, size, quality of personnel, extent of training	8.4	12.5	8.4	4.9	2.3

Thirty-five percent of the respondents identified company characteristics that made internal control unusually difficult to maintain at an adequate level. Table 5.19 ranks the characteristics most frequently cited, in descending order.

TABLE 5.19

**CFO RANKING OF COMPANY CHARACTERISTICS MAKING INTERNAL
CONTROL DIFFICULT**

Company Characteristic	**Frequency Count**
Decentralization	51
Geographic dispersion	47
Need for local management autonomy	38
Small size of staff	37
Diversity of business segments	31
Rapid growth of company or industry	30
Attitude of top management	22
Constant changes in products or services	18
Resistance by highly technical or creative personnel	13
Governmental regulation	12
Frequent acquisitions	10
Foreign operations	8
Too much rotation of personnel	6
Labour relations	6
Competitive management	6

Table 5.20 lists, in descending order, the type of transaction or activity within their company for which CFOs deemed adequate control most important.

TABLE 5.20

CFO RANKING OF ACTIVITIES MOST IMPORTANT TO INTERNAL CONTROL

Activities	Frequency Count
Cash disbursements	173
Cash receipts	119
Processing of computerized data	117
Purchasing	88
Inventory and materials handling	84
Payroll	60
Sales	59
International operations	24
Commissions, royalties or other variable payments	17
Other	7

Role of Internal Audit in Internal Control

CFOs were asked detailed questions about their internal audit departments. The range of topics covered included who received audit reports, the relationship between internal audit and the external auditors and the composition of the audit department staff.

The companies were characterized by certain internal control aspects such as:

Companies with internal audit functions	80.1%
Chief internal auditor provided with organizational independence	78.4%
Internal audit having access to board or corporate audit committee	72.9%
Companies having audit committees	79.5%
Companies having audit committees with employee members	29.5%
Internal control receiving more attention since audit committees emphasized	52.3%
Internal audit not given access to all areas of the firm	11.9%

The only areas of the company frequently not open to internal audit were senior management records such as salaries, confidential donations and other head office records.

Internal Control of Computerized Systems

CFOs were asked about the role of data processing in the organizational structure. Management was found to have:

Provided for general staff training in data processing for managers in the company not familiar with information systems	61.5%
Provided for a search for new computer applications to protect the company's competitive advantage	67.6%
A budget for finding new computer applications	41.8%
Established specific goals and objectives for computerized information systems	85.6%
A charge-back system for data processing costs	59.9%
Of those with a charge-back system — have a full-cost chargeback	74.0%
Provided for advancement opportunities within the company for the chief information officer	52.3%

Responsibility for Computerized Systems
Table 5.21 indicates (1) the organizational level that had primary responsibilities for specified activities and (2) other levels also responsible for the same tasks. CFOs stated that primary responsibility for computerized systems was generally divided between the chief financial officer/controller and the data processing manager. CFOs' responsibilities included:

• Assigning organizational responsibility for computerized systems.
• Responsibility for acquisition of computerized systems.

Data processing managers were held responsible for:
• Cost control over development and operations.
• Measuring efficiency and effectiveness of computerized systems.
• Assuring reliable computer security.
• Design of computerized systems.
• Responsibility for integrity of operating data.

The chief financial officer/controller and the data processing manager shared two areas of responsibility: (1) assuring that adequate internal controls were built into computerized systems and (2) authorizing changes to computerized systems.

TABLE 5.21

RESPONSIBILITY FOR COMPUTERIZED SYSTEMS BY PRIMARY AND OTHER RESPONSIBILITY LEVELS
(CFO Response)

	Managerial Level			
Responsibility	**Chief Financial Officer/ Controller (%)**	**Line Manager (%)**	**Internal Audit Manager (%)**	**Data Processing Manager (%)**
Assigning organizational responsibility for computerized systems	**51.7** 33.5	**12.7** 40.1	**0.4** 12.6	**32.2** 59.9
Responsibility for acquisition of computerized systems	**48.9** 43.0	**12.7** 35.0	**0.0** 12.0	**38.4** 57.0
Cost control over development and operations	**35.7** 48.8	**13.9** 37.4	**0.0** 5.4	**50.4** 46.8
Measuring efficiency and effectiveness of computerized systems	**30.8** 44.5	**18.6** 38.0	**7.6** 40.5	**43.0** 49.0
Assuring reliable computer security	**18.8** 51.0	**6.3** 30.5	**10.0** 55.0	**65.0** 31.5
Audit of data processing activities	**24.0** 47.1	**3.1** 15.9	**62.9** 19.6	**10.0** 60.9
Design of computerized systems	**9.4** 47.0	**13.6** 59.6	**0.4** 34.4	**76.6** 22.4
Responsibility for integrity of operating data	**25.8** 37.3	**26.7** 44.0	**0.8** 39.9	**46.6** 43.0
Assuring that adequate internal controls are built into computerized systems	**33.1** 44.2	**8.5** 37.4	**27.1** 48.5	**31.4** 56.8
Authorizing changes to computerized systems	**38.1** 37.8	**23.7** 37.2	**0.8** 30.1	**37.3** 55.1

Note: Primary levels of responsibility are in bold type and are reported using adjusted frequencies.

Risk

Table 5.22 reports CFOs' rankings of the strongest features of their companies' internal control systems. The four most important features, in rank order, were:

1. Formal control procedures such as separation of duties, independent reviews, reconciliations, and evaluations.
2. Attitude of top management.

3. Control measures specifically designed for the most sensitive or otherwise important control measures.
4. Quality of personnel.

TABLE 5.22

STRONGEST FEATURES OF INTERNAL CONTROL SYSTEMS (CFO Response)

	Rankings				
Features	**Strongest 1 (%)**	**2 (%)**	**3 (%)**	**4 (%)**	**Fifth Strongest 5 (%)**
Control measures specifically designed for our most sensitive or otherwise important control problems	19.0	11.0	9.5	6.8	8.0
Company traditions and customs	5.7	4.6	8.0	8.7	6.5
Quality of our personnel	11.0	12.2	12.5	10.6	6.8
Attitude of top management	18.3	12.2	14.4	10.6	11.0
Special attention to electronic data processing controls	2.3	3.4	8.7	8.7	9.9
Monitoring of compliance with internal control measures	4.9	8.0	10.3	16.0	15.2
A widespread awareness that control measures exist	6.5	9.9	11.8	10.6	14.1
Formal control procedures such as separation of duties, independent reviews, reconciliations and evaluations	23.2	18.6	7.2	12.9	8.4
An active internal audit department	5.3	15.6	12.9	7.6	9.5

Table 5.23 presents assessments of risk, from an internal control perspective. In overall rank order, chief financial officers found the five greatest areas of internal control risk to be:

1. Electronic data processing.
2. Inventory, receiving, shipping and materials handling.
3. Decentralized operations.
4. Product pricing.
5. Purchasing

TABLE 5.23

**INTERNAL CONTROL RISKS BY DEGREE OF CONCERN
(CFO Response)**

Risks	Degree of Concern		
	Of Major Concern (%)	Of Some Concern (%)	Not a Concern (%)
Decentralized operations	18.5	46.2	35.3
Electronic data processing	32.4	54.0	13.6
Production quality control	8.1	30.3	61.5
Foreign operations	6.4	22.6	71.1
Purchasing	11.8	53.5	34.7
Marketing	8.3	37.1	54.6
Budgeting	9.8	40.8	49.4
Research and development	2.1	18.6	79.3
Compliance with government regulations	9.7	36.8	53.4
Financing activities	10.7	34.0	55.3
External financial reporting	6.6	23.7	69.7
Inventory, receiving, shipping and materials handling	22.1	44.7	33.2
Construction and contracting	11.1	29.5	59.4
Product pricing	17.3	44.9	37.9
Payroll	12.3	31.1	56.6
Investment	12.0	27.3	60.7
New or greatly expanding company operations	17.8	34.7	47.5
Others	5.9	23.5	70.6

CFOs' assessment of potential risks associated with computerized operations are detailed in Table 5.24. The five potential risks that ranked highest were:

1. Monitoring effectiveness and efficiency of computerized systems.
2. Maintaining an adequate audit trail.
3. Having a recovery plan in case of hardware destruction (tied for third).
4. Ability to audit the actual program (tied for third).
5. Testing of such a recovery program.

TABLE 5.24

**COMPUTERIZED SYSTEMS' RISKS BY EXTENT OF PROBLEM
(CFO Response)**

	Extent of Problem		
Risks	**A Significant Potential Problem (%)**	**A Minor Problem (%)**	**Not A Problem (%)**
Maintaining an adequate audit trail	33.2	43.0	23.8
Ability to audit the actual programs	29.5	47.8	22.7
Not sufficiently involving internal audit with the establishment of data processing systems	21.3	43.1	35.6
Ability of internal audit to audit data processing operations	20.8	40.7	38.6
Ability of external audit to audit data processing operations	11.2	40.2	48.6
Locating data processing personnel with sufficient expertise	15.2	46.4	38.4
Not sufficiently involving operating management with establishment of data processing systems	21.8	44.0	34.1
Cost control of data processing operations	25.3	40.7	34.0
Monitoring effectiveness and efficiency of computerized systems	33.1	49.0	17.9
Transmission of computerized data over telephone or satellite	11.3	36.8	51.8
Having a recovery plan in case of hardware destruction	35.7	35.3	28.9
Testing of such a recovery program	34.0	36.8	29.2

Internal Control and the External Auditor

Most CFOs were generally satisfied with the service provided by their external auditors. Percentages satisfied with the following were:

Audit of financial information	97.3%
Audit of computerized systems	79.7%

Of those expressing dissatisfaction, reasons cited included:
• Lack of EDP expertise.
• External audit not well staffed.
• Would like more contribution — not enough detail.
• Not enough time.

Internal Control and Industry Influences

When companies were broken down by industry, considerable differences in internal control practices were identified. Table 5.25 presents industry data for several internal control practices.

TABLE 5.25

INTERNAL CONTROL CHARACTERISTICS BY INDUSTRY
(CFO Response)

Companies having:	Industry							
	Retailing (%)	Transportation (%)	Manufacturing (%)	Forestry (%)	Mining (%)	Utilities (%)	Petroleum & Energy (%)	Finance (%)
A written code of conduct	77.8	33.3	64.9	55.6	42.9	80.0	63.2	75.6
An internal audit function	88.9	66.7	84.4	44.4	85.7	93.3	88.9	91.3
Staff training in data processing for managers unfamiliar with EDP	77.8	83.3	60.0	22.2	14.3	93.3	66.7	54.3
Search for new computer applications to protect company advantage	88.9	66.7	68.0	77.8	42.9	60.0	72.2	73.9
Specific goals for EDP	88.9	83.3	90.8	66.7	85.7	92.9	83.3	78.3
Inconsistent quality of internal control	55.6	66.7	54.7	77.8	57.1	46.7	68.4	60.9
Company characteristics making internal control hard to maintain	44.6	33.3	29.7	66.7	16.7	20.0	22.2	43.2
An audit committee	93.8	90.0	78.9	80.0	100.0	88.9	88.9	93.3
Company employees on audit committee	50.0	50.0	35.2	60.0	33.3	11.1	38.9	25.0

The contention of top utility officers that regulation was a positive factor in promoting good internal control was borne out by the above results, showing a particularly good performance for utilities on all the preceding indicators. The only exception was the somewhat small provision for an ongoing search for new computer applications to protect the company's advantage. Because utilities are legal monopolies, this difference could be explained by their not having to compete in the same way as other industries.

Mining firms appeared to find that their companies' characteristics made internal control easier to maintain than did most other companies. Forestry companies, for reasons that are unclear from this data, found that their companies had characteristics making internal control difficult to maintain. Forestry companies also showed the highest percentage of company employees on their audit committees and a lower percentage of companies providing staff training in data processing for managers. For the latter, however, it is likely that the nature of forestry operations reduces the requirement for managerial personnel to be trained in computerized systems.

Transportation companies reported the lowest percentage of written codes of conduct, as well as the highest percentage of inconsistencies in quality of internal control throughout their companies. As a group, however, they did not see their companies as having characteristics making it unusually difficult to maintain adequate internal control.

US Foreign Corrupt Practices Act

Companies required to comply with the US FCPA were 28.2 percent. Specific actions taken to comply with this act included issuing specific policy statements, developing a code of conduct, informing key personnel, having them sign a statement, filling in a questionnaire from the parent and documenting the system.

Eleven percent of the companies were wrestling with particular internal control problems. No problems appeared to be widespread. There were a few comments about each type of problem, primarily on purchasing, sales, levels of control over data processing, and controlling research and development expenses.

INTERNAL AUDIT MANAGER RESPONSES

The following section provides data from the internal audit manager questionnaires.

Communication of Internal Control Policies

Internal audit managers were asked how their companies communicated internal control measures and practices to employees. They reported that their companies' acknowledgment of the existence of a control system by reference to it in policy letters, management statements, delegation of authority and job description was:

Extensive	51.5%
To some extent	45.8%
Not at all	2.6%

As shown in Table 5.26, a majority of companies informed their employees about company objectives, personal responsibilities and applicable internal control areas. The emphasis was on the communication of internal control information to officers and key employees of the firm.

TABLE 5.26

**COMMUNICATION OF INTERNAL CONTROL INFORMATION BY
EMPLOYEE CATEGORY
(Internal Audit Manager Response)**

	Employee Category	
	Officers and Key Employees (%)	Others (%)
Information		
Company objectives	86.2	53.9
Their personal responsibilities	85.8	76.7
Applicable internal control measures	70.7	56.5

The internal audit managers characterized their firms' manuals as providing descriptions of internal control as follows:

Complete	6.6%
Almost complete	24.8%
Partial	41.2%
Very little	25.7%
Other (e.g., manuals just completed)	1.8%

Objectives of Internal Control

Table 5.27 provides data on perceptions of the importance of internal control objectives within the company. The resulting rank order of the ten objectives of internal control was:

1. Safeguarding of assets.
2. Ensuring reliability of accounting records.
3. Prevention and detection of error.
4. Ensuring compliance with management policies.
5. Ensuring orderly and efficient conduct of business.

  6. Prevention and detection of fraud.
  7. Profitability and minimization of costs.
  8. Assuring effective use of company resources.
  9. Discharging statutory responsibility to owners.
10. Timely preparation of financial statements.

TABLE 5.27

**PERCEPTION OF INTERNAL CONTROL OBJECTIVES BY DEGREE OF
IMPORTANCE
(Internal Audit Manager Response)**

	Degree of Importance			
Objectives	**Very Important (%)**	**Somewhat Important (%)**	**Of Little Importance (%)**	**Not Important (%)**
Prevention and detection of fraud	59.9	37.4	2.6	0.0
Prevention and detection of error	75.4	23.2	1.3	0.0
Ensuring orderly and efficient conduct of business	68.7	28.6	2.2	0.4
Discharging statutory responsibilities to owners	51.6	37.3	8.0	3.1
Safeguarding assets	91.2	8.3	0.4	0.0
Profitability and minimization of costs	59.5	33.0	6.6	0.9
Assuring effective use of company resources	58.8	32.9	7.0	1.3
Ensuring reliability of accounting records	86.0	13.2	0.9	0.0
Timely preparation of financial statements	42.5	46.5	9.7	1.3
Ensuring compliance with management policies	70.5	28.6	0.9	0.0

Responsibility for Internal Control Systems

Companies that clearly stated the responsibilities of different positions and levels of authority in their manuals or instructions comprised 60.8 percent.

Responsibility for Reporting

Table 5.28 indicates the organizational level(s) where various responsibilities for internal control systems were concentrated. The controller or chief accounting officer was assigned the primary responsibility for designing the internal control system. The CFO, CEO and audit committee or board were reported as having the responsibility for approving the system. Responsibility for the evaluation of systems' effectiveness was assigned primarily to the external and internal auditors. The CFO, controller/chief accounting officer and CEO were the major participants in authorizing changes to the internal control system.

TABLE 5.28

MANAGERIAL LEVEL BY SYSTEMS RESPONSIBILITY
(Internal Audit Manager Response)

	Responsibility			
Managerial Level	**Designs Internal Control System (%)**	**Approves the System (%)**	**Evaluates Systems' Effectiveness (%)**	**Authorizes Changes to the System (%)**
Chief financial officer	16.9	79.7	15.7	65.7
Controller or chief accounting officer	79.0	44.3	20.0	60.0
Internal audit manager	19.2	14.1	95.8	9.4
Chief executive officer	2.2	70.0	8.9	52.2
External auditor	4.6	6.5	96.7	2.0
Audit committee or board	0.0	51.6	43.5	29.0

Table 5.29 details managerial reporting responsibilities. Internal audit managers stated that the responsibility for reporting on internal control to both financial management and senior management was primarily theirs. The external auditor was most often designated as having responsibility for reporting on internal control to the board or audit committee. The data processing managers reported most frequently to the CFO.

TABLE 5.29

MANAGERIAL REPORTING RESPONSIBILITIES BY REPORT
(Internal Audit Manager Response)

	Responsibility			
Managerial Level	**Reports on Internal Control to Financial Management (%)**	**Reports on Internal Control to Senior Management (%)**	**Reports on Internal Control to Board or Audit Committee (%)**	**Receives Data Processing Manager's Report (%)**
Chief executive officer	21.4	30.1	67.0	35.9
Chief financial officer	31.9	56.3	56.9	66.9
Controller	66.7	58.7	25.3	41.3
Internal audit	83.4	88.1	65.3	23.8
External audit	69.3	76.0	76.0	8.9
Line manager	58.2	49.4	10.1	39.2

Those groups receiving internal audit's reports were:

Auditee	98.1%
Chief financial officer	96.1%
Auditee's vice-president	94.1%
External auditor	89.1%
Audit committee	59.7%
Other	48.7%

The "Other" category included recipients of the audit report such as: chief executive officer and president (3.4 percent), senior management in general (30.5 percent) and the auditee's president or supervisor (5.9 percent).

Budgeting
Table 5.30 indicates the extent to which certain types of expenditures were controlled by budgets, together with the level of approval required to exceed limits. A majority of firms had a budgeted amount or a fixed maximum amount that could only be exceeded by the approval of the full board, senior management or a senior officer.

TABLE 5.30

EXPENDITURE CATEGORY BY EXTENT OF BUDGETING CONTROLS AND APPROVAL LEVEL
(Internal Audit Manager Response)

	Nature of Limit			
Expenditure Category	None (%)	Budgeted Amount (%)	Fixed Maximum Amount (%)	Level of Approval Required to Exceed Limit
Operating expenditures	9.7	76.3	14.0	Senior officer
Inventory purchases	25.1	54.5	20.4	Senior officer
Capital expenditures	0.9	62.7	36.3	Full board
Incurrence of debt:				
Under one year	20.0	41.7	38.3	Full board or senior management
More than one year	16.2	34.7	49.1	Full board or senior management
Contracts to sell or provide a service	32.2	39.2	28.7	Full board or senior management

Cost-Benefit Analyses of Internal Control Systems Changes
The following types of cost-benefit analyses were undertaken before introducing significant changes to the internal control system:

Formal analysis	14.6%
Informal analysis	72.1%
No analysis	13.2%

Compliance Monitoring of Internal Control
A question measuring whether firms practised compliance monitoring of inter-

nal control procedures indicated that companies that provided for such monitoring composed 81.9 percent of the sample. The percentage of managers who assessed their compliance monitoring as excessive, about right or less than desirable was:

Excessive	1.7%
About right	71.1%
Less than desirable	18.1%

Compliance monitoring was provided by the following:

Internal audit function	88.8%
Controller's department	55.6%
Systems specialist	16.4%
Independent external auditors	65.5%
Others	8.6%

The "Others" in this question included line management, senior management, federal government auditors and outside consultants. The above data further support the importance within the firm of the internal audit function.

Rating of Systems
Table 5.31 reports the respondents' self-assessment of their firms' internal control systems, internal audit systems and internal audit of computerized systems. Of the total, 29.7 per cent of the internal audit managers rated their internal control systems as either excellent or approaching excellence. The percentage of internal audit managers who ranked their own internal audit systems as excellent or approaching excellence was 37.8. For internal audit of computerized systems, however, only 15.3 percent of internal audit managers ranked their systems as excellent or approaching excellence. This evidence was repeated in a variety of ways throughout the study, providing support for the identification of a major internal control concern.

TABLE 5.31

ASSESSMENT OF INTERNAL CONTROL BY SYSTEM
(Internal Audit Manager Response)

	System		
Rating	**Internal Control System (%)**	**Internal Audit System (%)**	**Internal Audit of Computerized System (%)**
Excellent — includes all measures that can be justified	12.6	9.2	1.9
Approaching excellence — final improvements are either in process of implementation or under consideration	17.1	28.6	13.4
Satisfactory — needs minor improvement	63.5	50.2	43.1
Needs major improvement	6.3	9.7	37.0

Consistency of Internal Control

When asked about the consistency of internal control and the characteristics that make internal control difficult, internal audit managers reported the following:

Inconsistency existing in internal control	57.6%
Specific characteristics existing that made internal control difficult	48.3%

Characteristics making internal control difficult ranked by reported frequency are reported in Table 5.32.

TABLE 5.32

**INTERNAL AUDIT MANAGER RANKING OF
COMPANY CHARACTERISTICS
MAKING INTERNAL CONTROL DIFFICULT**

Company Characteristic	Frequency Count
Geographic dispersion	61
Decentralization	52
Need for local management autonomy	38
Small size of staff	38
Rapid growth of company or industry	34
Attitude of top management	27
Diversity of business segments	25
Too much rotation of personnel	21
Resistance by highly technical or creative personnel	20
Constant changes in products or services	18
Frequent acquisitions	15
Government regulation	13
Labour relations	12
Foreign operations	11
Competitive management	7

Table 5.33 lists the type of transactions or activities within the respondents' companies for which adequate internal control was deemed important by frequency count.

TABLE 5.33

**INTERNAL AUDIT MANAGER RANKING OF ACTIVITIES
MOST IMPORTANT TO CONTROL**

Activity	Frequency Count
Cash disbursements	144
Processing of computerized data	116
Cash receipts	99
Inventory and materials handling	75
Purchasing	72
Sales	57
Payroll	45
International operations	19
Commission, royalty or other variable payments	12

Role of Internal Audit in Internal Control

An investigation of the role of internal audit and audit committees indicated the following:

Firms with audit committees	84.6%
Internal audit function having access to board or corporate audit committee	69.3%
Companies with employees as audit committee members	34.1%
Companies where internal control received more attention since emphasis on audit committees increased	65.8%
Chief internal auditor had organizational independence (that is, not dependent for job, pay, or promotion purpose) from those responsible for the activities audited	78.9%
Companies with areas of their firms not open to the internal audit department	17.9%

The most commonly listed areas not open to inspection were payroll and the executive payroll (63.5 percent of those responding affirmatively), subsidiaries abroad, head office and pension plans.

Internal audit managers reported those approving their annual audit programs were:

Chief financial officer	81.1%
Audit committee	70.1%
External audit	33.3%
Other	77.1%

Included in the category of "Other" were the chief executive officer (21.6 percent), senior management including the position of president (15 percent), parent's internal audit department (8.1 percent) and "not formally approved" (5.4 percent).

The relationship between the internal audit department and the auditee was reported as follows:

Auditee was consulted prior to the beginning of the audit and allowed to make specific requests	85.0%
Auditee was consulted prior to audit report's completion	97.7%
Auditee had option of disagreeing with findings or recommendations	92.8%
Auditee was required to follow up the audit report	80.2%

Methods of evaluation of internal audit's performance were:

Feedback from auditees	92.8%
Judgment of chief financial officer	89.2%
Company savings achieved	50.7%
Audits by parent	32.1%
Other	34.1%

"Other" included external auditors, the audit committee and senior management other than the CFO.

Only 17.5 percent of internal audit managers said they were dissatisfied with the evaluation process. Primary reasons given for dissatisfaction included:
- Their firms had no performance appraisals.
- Criteria were not defined.
- There was a general lack of feedback.

Internal audit's resources were employed on the following activities:

Operational audit	38.9%
Financial statement information	27.4%
Computerized systems	21.1%
Special audits	14.4%
All other areas, not identified	23.1%

Internal audit managers stated that the internal audit function was perceived as being both policing and consulting roles in most firms. Their assessments were as reported below:

Seen as a policeman	61.6%
Seen as a consultant	74.6%

Internal audit managers were generally satisfied with this perception (60.3 percent). Reasons given for satisfaction were:
- It is the accepted role.
- Maintains professional standards.
- We are internal control consultants.
- We represent an important management tool.
- Internal audit provides the auditee with good feedback.

Internal Control of Computerized Systems

Responsibility for Computerized Systems
Table 5.34 provides data for (1) the organizational level that had primary responsibility for certain tasks and (2) other levels that were also responsible for the same tasks. The data processing manager was thought to have primary responsibility for:
- Cost control over development and operations.
- Measuring efficiency and effectiveness of computerized systems.

- Assuring reliable computer security.
- Design of computerized systems.
- Sign-offs of computerized systems.
- Responsibility for integrity of operating data.
- Assuring that adequate internal controls are built into computerized systems.

The chief financial officer/controller was thought to have primary responsibility for assigning organizational responsibility for computerized systems. The internal audit manager was stated to have primary responsibility for auditing data processing activities while the line manager and data processing manager were responsible for authorizing changes to computerized systems.

TABLE 5.34

**RESPONSIBILITY FOR COMPUTERIZED SYSTEMS
BY PRIMARY AND OTHER RESPONSIBILITY LEVELS
(Internal Audit Manager Response)**

	Managerial Level			
Responsibility	**Chief Financial Officer/ Controller (%)**	**Line Manager (%)**	**Internal Audit Manager (%)**	**Data Processing Manager (%)**
Assigning organizational responsibility for computerized systems	**57.1** 23.3	**11.0** 32.5	**0.5** 12.9	**31.5** 60.7
Cost control over development and operations	**40.5** 42.2	**15.5** 36.8	**0.0** 15.7	**44.1** 43.8
Measuring efficiency and effectiveness of computerized systems	**23.3** 29.7	**15.5** 35.4	**13.2** 62.0	**47.9** 40.6
Assuring reliable computer security	**11.7** 36.9	**5.8** 27.8	**9.4** 75.9	**73.1** 23.0
Audit of data processing activities	**8.4** 35.3	**0.5** 28.6	**83.7** 16.8	**7.4** 68.9
Design of computerized systems	**11.3** 36.4	**12.7** 59.7	**0.0** 46.0	**76.0** 22.7
Sign-offs of computerized systems	**16.4** 28.8	**38.8** 34.1	**2.3** 48.8	**42.5** 51.2
Responsibility for integrity of operating data	**24.1** 29.1	**35.0** 38.5	**0.9** 53.1	**40.0** 50.8
Assuring that adequate internal controls are built into computerized systems	**20.3** 36.1	**14.7** 40.3	**24.9** 67.0	**40.1** 50.3
Authorizing changes to computerized systems	**31.7** 32.6	**33.9** 31.1	**0.9** 32.1	**33.5** 57.4

Note: Primary levels of responsibility are in bold type and are reported using adjusted frequencies.

Risk

Table 5.35 reports rankings of the five strongest internal control features in the respondents' companies. The five most important features (from Table 5.35), in rank order were:

1. Formal control procedures such as separation of duties, independent reviews, reconciliations and evaluations.
2. Control measures specifically designed for our most sensitive or otherwise important control measures.
3. Attitude of top management (tied for third).
4. An active internal audit department (tied for third).
5. Quality of personnel

TABLE 5.35

STRONGEST FEATURES OF INTERNAL CONTROL SYSTEMS BY RANK
(Internal Audit Manager Response)

	Rankings				
Features	**Strongest 1 (%)**	**2 (%)**	**3 (%)**	**4 (%)**	**Fifth Strongest 5 (%)**
Control measures specifically designed for our most sensitive or otherwise important control problems	13.8	13.4	6.5	12.1	6.0
Company traditions and customs	3.0	3.4	7.8	4.7	6.5
Quality of our personnel	10.3	9.9	12.1	12.5	6.5
Attitude of top management	12.1	12.1	9.5	12.1	12.9
Special attention to electronic data processing controls	1.7	5.6	6.5	7.3	8.6
Monitoring of compliance with internal control measures	2.6	10.3	13.8	10.3	22.0
A widespread awareness that control measures exist	5.2	6.0	11.2	11.2	13.8
Formal control procedures such as separation of duties, independent reviews, reconciliations, and evaluations	37.1	16.4	9.5	13.4	6.0
An active internal audit department	12.1	19.4	19.8	12.9	12.5

Table 5.36 presents assessed perceptions of risk. In overall rank order, the five greatest areas of internal control risk were:
1. Electronic data processing.
2. Inventory, receiving, shipping and materials handling.

3. New or greatly expanding company operations.
4. Purchasing.
5. Decentralized operations.

TABLE 5.36

INTERNAL CONTROL RISKS BY DEGREE OF CONCERN
(Internal Audit Manager Response)

Risks	Degree of Concern		
	Of Major Concern (%)	Of Some Concern (%)	Not a Concern (%)
Decentralized operations	19.5	43.0	37.6
Electronic data processing	53.6	40.2	6.3
Production quality control	9.0	32.7	58.3
Foreign operations	6.6	23.7	69.7
Purchasing	22.3	49.5	28.2
Marketing	14.8	40.7	44.4
Budgeting	9.6	45.9	44.5
Research and development	2.4	16.5	81.1
Compliance with government regulations	11.9	43.6	44.5
Financing activities	15.2	40.6	44.2
External financial reporting	8.8	37.2	54.0
Inventory, receiving, shipping and materials handling	34.9	39.0	26.1
Construction and contracting	19.6	31.8	48.6
Product pricing	13.5	39.1	47.4
Payroll	14.1	51.4	34.5
Investment	15.4	33.6	50.9
New or greatly expanding company operations	23.7	38.4	37.9
Others	20.6	8.8	70.6

Internal audit managers' rank order of perceptions of potential risks associated with computerized operations within their firms are presented in Table 5.37. The five potential risks that ranked highest were:

1. Maintaining an adequate audit trail.
2. Testing of such a recovery program.
3. Monitoring effectiveness and efficiency of computerized systems.
4. Ability to audit the actual program.
5. Having a recovery plan in case of hardware destruction.

TABLE 5.37

COMPUTERIZED SYSTEMS' RISKS BY EXTENT OF PROBLEM
(Internal Audit Manager Response)

Risks	Extent of Problem		
	A Significant Potential Problem (%)	A Minor Problem (%)	Not A Problem (%)
Maintaining an adequate audit trail	47.7	37.7	14.5
Ability to audit the actual programs	45.0	35.0	20.0
Not sufficiently involving internal audit with the establishment of data processing systems	33.5	44.3	22.2
Ability of internal audit to audit data processing operations	33.6	32.7	33.6
Ability of external audit to audit data processing operations	18.6	44.1	37.3
Locating internal audit personnel with sufficient expertise	24.8	44.5	30.7
Restricting access to computer information	33.6	39.5	26.9
Cost control of data processing operations	30.2	46.4	23.4
Monitoring effectiveness and efficiency of computerized systems	42.1	44.8	13.1
Transmission of computerized data over telephone or satellite	24.1	40.5	35.5
Ensuring access and security of computer facilities and backup files	32.3	42.6	25.1
Keeping backup files current	15.7	40.4	43.9
Having a recovery plan in case of hardware destruction	43.5	35.4	21.1
Testing of such a recovery program	45.7	38.5	15.8

Firms classifying computerized data according to its sensitivity and, instituting controls accordingly were 68.2 percent.

Internal Control and the External Auditor

In 83.1 percent of the cases, the external auditors were said to rely on work performed by the internal auditor. In 57 percent of these cases, this reliance was estimated to have reduced fees charged the firm by external auditors on average 16.2 percent.

When asked to evaluate the performance of their external auditors, internal audit managers were:

Satisfied with audits of financial information	89.7%
Satisfied with external audit's ability to audit computer operations	49.6%

Reasons given for dissatisfaction with external auditing of computer operations included:
• Lack of EDP expertise.
• No computer work performed.

- External audit lacks the time and resources to audit EDP.
- External audit of computer operations is too superficial.
- External audit must rely on internal audit for audit of computer facilities.

DATA PROCESSING MANAGER RESPONSES

This section reports results from the data processing managers' questionnaire.

Communication of Internal Control Policies

Data processing managers were asked about the extent to which companies acknowledged the existence of a control system by referring to it in policy letters, management statements, delegation of authority and job descriptions. They assessed their companies' references as:

Extensive	31.2%
To some extent	62.7%
Not at all	6.1%

Table 5.38 provides data on whether a comprehensive effort was made to convey internal control practices to specific groups of employees. Data processing managers reported that their companies informed both groups of employees about objectives, personal responsibilities and other internal control areas, but employees other than officers and key employees received less information about company objectives and internal control measures.

TABLE 5.38

**COMMUNICATION OF INTERNAL CONTROL INFORMATION BY EMPLOYEE CATEGORY
(Data Processing Manager Responses)**

	Employee Category	
	Officers and Key Employees	Others
Information	(%)	(%)
Company objectives	82.5	47.0
Their personal responsibilities	81.0	74.6
Applicable internal control measures	70.9	59.7

The respondents were asked how complete the company manuals were in describing the firm's internal control systems. Assessments are presented below:

Complete description	8.3%
Almost complete	18.6%
Partial	36.7%
Very little	33.3%
Other (e.g., manuals just completed)	3.0%

Less than 27 percent of data processing managers characterized their firms' manuals as providing complete or almost complete descriptions. A substantial minority appeared to have very little documentation.

Responsibility for Internal Control Systems

Budgeting
In an investigation of the data processing department's budget, data processing managers reported the following activities:

Operating departments participated in the budget planning process for computerized information systems	59.9%
Actual results were compared with budget	89.5%
Material differences were documented	78.5%

Those who received explanations of material budget differences were:

Board of directors	14.6%
Corporate management	66.4%
Divisional management	57.8%
Unit or department management	53.7%

Management by exception appeared to be alive and well in these instances.

Cost-Benefit Analyses of Internal Control Systems Change
In examining whether cost-benefit analyses were undertaken before introducing significant changes to the internal control system, the types of cost-benefit analyses reported were:

Formal analysis	26.3%
Informal analysis	58.4%
No analysis	15.3%

Responsibility for Reporting
In examining whether data processing managers had reporting responsibilities to more than one individual, the percentage of those receiving data processing managers' reports was found to be:

Chief executive officer	13.1%
Chief financial officer	51.1%
Controller	12.7%
Other	24.3%

"Other" included the following: vice president, corporate planning; vice president, Management Information Systems; parent firm's MIS director; and the MIS steering committee. The percentage of those receiving data processing's reports on internal control was:

Senior management	74.6%
Internal audit	24.6%
External audit	20.5%
Other	4.9%

The "Other" responses to this question included their firm's MIS steering committee; parent's MIS director, manager, or vice president; or that they did not report to anyone on internal control.

Compliance Monitoring of Internal Control
When determining whether firms monitored compliance with internal control procedures, companies providing for monitoring of procedures were 69.4 percent. The percentage of data processing managers who assessed their companies compliance monitoring as excessive, about right, or less than desirable was:

Excessive	1.5%
About right	58.2%
Less than desirable	14.9%

Those providing companies' compliance monitoring were:

Internal audit function	61.6%
Controller's department	31.3%
Systems specialist	29.1%
Independent external auditors	45.9%
Others	5.2%

"Others" in this question included management review, systems management and parent company's auditors.

Rating of Systems
Table 5.39 shows how data processing managers assessed their departments' internal control systems, external audit of computerized systems and the internal audit of their computerized systems. Their own departments' internal control systems were rated as either excellent or approaching excellence by only 25.7 percent of data processing managers. External audit of computerized systems was ranked as excellent or approaching excellence by only 15.7 percent of data processing managers. For internal audit of computerized systems, only 16.1 percent of data processing managers ranked their systems as excellent or approaching excellence. These data are additional evidence supporting the finding that there is difficulty in controlling and evaluating EDP operations.

TABLE 5.39

ASSESSMENT OF INTERNAL CONTROL BY SYSTEM
(Data Processing Manager Response)

	System		
Ratings	Internal Control System (%)	External Audit of Computerized System (%)	Internal Audit of Computerized System (%)
Excellent — includes all measures that can be justified	8.6	5.8	5.5
Approaching excellence — final improvements are either in process of implementation or under consideration	17.1	9.9	10.6
Satisfactory — needs minor improvement	57.6	58.7	44.7
Needs major improvement	16.0	23.6	37.9

Consistency of Internal Control

Data on the consistency of internal control and characteristics that may make internal control difficult was provided by data processing managers who stated that:

Inconsistency in internal control of computerized systems existed	54.2%
Specific characteristics made internal control of departments difficult to maintain at an adequate level	45.1%

These characteristics were ranked in order of frequency in Table 5.40.

TABLE 5.40

DATA PROCESSING MANAGER RANKING OF COMPANY
CHARACTERISTICS MAKING INTERNAL CONTROL DIFFICULT

Company Characteristic	Frequency Count
Geographic dispersion	59
Decentralization	51
Small size of staff	49
Need for local management autonomy	43
Rapid growth of company or industry	41
Attitude of top management	32
Diversity of business segments	29
Frequent acquisitions	22
Resistance by highly technical or creative personnel	20
Constant changes in products or services	17
Competitive management	15
Too much rotation of personnel	12
Foreign operations	7
Governmental regulation	6
Labour relations	2

Role of Internal Audit in Internal Control

When asked how internal audit was perceived within the firm, it was found that the internal auditor was viewed most often as a consultant (62.3 percent), much less as a policeman (39.2 percent) and as a management spy in only 6 percent of data processing managers' responses.

Internal Control of Computerized Systems

Data processing managers were asked specific questions about data processing's role in the firm. The range of topics included several aspects of the organizational roles of data processing managers and their departments.

Firms having coordinating committees for computerized systems	69.8%
Training provided in data processing for managers unfamiliar with computerized information systems	46.8%
Search for new computer applications is undertaken	67.4%
Budget provided to search for new computer applications	36.4%
Charge-back system used for data processing costs	57.3%
Full-cost charge-back system used	54.1%
A specific job description exists for data processing manager	83.6%
Responsibilities and level of authority for different positions are clearly stated in company manuals	63.5%
Advancement opportunities within the firm have been provided for the data processing manager	31.6%
Specific goals and objectives have been established for computerized information systems	83.5%

Performance Evaluation of Data Processing
When evaluation of the data processing department was addressed, it was found

that most companies used multiple criteria. The percentages of criteria used in the evaluation of the data processing department were:

Operating departments	91.8%
Judgment of immediate superior	85.8%
Development of new applications	80.2%
Keeping within budget	72.8%
Financial management	72.4%
External auditors	66.0%
Internal audit	57.8%
Judgment of CEO	51.1%
Other	11.2%

The most frequent explanation under "Other" was that data processing was being measured against objectives set by management. Of those responding, 70.8 percent were satisfied with the way they were being evaluated. Those who were dissatisfied gave the following reasons:

- Tendency of management to forget good news and concentrate on bad news.
- Judgments not based on solid EDP knowledge.
- Not enough requirements for performance to be measured against objectives.
- Costs for the enhancement of installed systems not really understood.
- Often data processing is measured on projects but has no full authority over user resources.
- User evaluations often based on misconceptions about data processing's role and their role in supporting data processing's efforts.

Although data processing managers appeared to receive less internal assistance than they might wish, 60.2 percent reported receiving trade journals that discussed special adaptations of the computer to their industry problems.

Responsibility for Computerized Systems
Table 5.41 reports the assessment of aspects of computerized systems. The table designates: (1) the organizational level that had primary responsibility for specified activities and (2) other levels that were also responsible for the same activities. The CFO's primary responsibility was identified as assigning organizational responsibility for computerized systems. Line managers were primarily involved in sign-offs of computerized systems as well as authorizing changes to computerized systems. Besides auditing, internal audit was involved in helping to ensure that adequate internal controls were built into computerized systems. As anticipated, data processing was heavily involved in almost every activity. Although trends are identifiable in the responses, there is involvement across all levels of the organization for almost every activity. This is further evidence of the diffuse nature of computerized information processing in today's corporations.

TABLE 5.41

RESPONSIBILITIES FOR COMPUTERIZED SYSTEMS BY PRIMARY AND OTHER RESPONSIBILITY LEVELS
(Data Processing Manager Response)

	Managerial Level			
Responsibility	**Chief Financial Officer/ Controller (%)**	**Line Manager (%)**	**Internal Audit Manager (%)**	**Data Processing Manager (%)**
Assigning organizational responsibility for computerized systems	**44.4** 29.3	**0.0** 46.3	**10.9** 11.2	**44.7** 55.6
Cost control over development and operations	**11.5** 57.3	**4.2** 48.2	**0.0** 12.1	**84.4** 18.1
Responsibility for acquisition of computerized systems	**17.4** 57.3	**8.0** 49.1	**0.0** 9.5	**74.6** 25.9
Assimilating computerized systems into the company	**6.6** 41.9	**14.7** 62.7	**0.4** 18.4	**78.4** 24.4
Measuring efficiency and effectiveness of computerized systems	**5.4** 34.2	**14.9** 52.9	**1.5** 38.0	**78.2** 25.1
Assuring reliable computer security	**5.0** 38.5	**3.4** 35.4	**4.6** 58.9	**87.0** 14.6
Audit of data processing activities	**12.1** 44.6	**2.0** 24.9	**64.8** 14.7	**21.1** 67.2
Design of computerized systems	**1.1** 28.5	**11.4** 74.0	**0.4** 36.0	**87.1** 13.0
Sign-offs of computerized systems	**5.5** 27.4	**60.5** 29.4	**0.4** 35.8	**33.6** 63.2
Responsibility for integrity of operating data	**6.9** 24.5	**29.5** 47.4	**1.9** 37.5	**61.7** 42.3
Assuring that adequate internal controls are built into computerized systems	**8.9** 31.4	**9.3** 51.6	**23.6** 42.6	**58.3** 42.2
Authorizing changes to computerized systems	**10.7** 27.7	**46.4** 36.9	**0.4** 23.8	**42.5** 57.3

Note: Primary levels of responsibility are in bold type and are reported using adjusted frequencies.

Ranking and Rating of Computerized Systems

Computerization of respondents' firms was ranked against others in their industry. Managers ranked extent of their firm's computerization compared to others as:

Substantially greater	5.2%
Somewhat greater	28.4%
About the same	41.4%
Somewhat less	19.8%
Substantially less	4.5%

When companies were categorized and analyzed by size, smaller companies were found to have significantly less computerization (.04 level) by a one-way analysis of variance.

A majority of respondents rated their current data processing hardware and software as either capable of meeting anticipated needs or sufficient to meet present needs. When analyzed by industry, mining companies indicated a greater concern than companies in other industries about their hardware becoming obsolete (57.1 percent). Only 13.6 percent of the financial institutions were concerned about obsolescence.

TABLE 5.42

RATING OF COMPUTERIZED SYSTEMS BY HARDWARE AND SOFTWARE NEEDS
(Data Processing Manager Response)

Ratings	Hardware (%)	Software (%)
Capable of meeting anticipated needs over the next five years	23.1	25.7
Sufficient to meet present needs	74.3	65.7
Becoming obsolete	26.5	38.1
Obsolete	3.7	6.3

Reliance on Computer
The extent of companies' reliance on the computer for corporate activities is shown in Table 5.43. The areas of financial and accounting data, inventory and operations were found to rely most heavily on the computer. When categorized by industry, there were significant differences (.05 level) concerning the extent of reliance on computers for operations, inventory and engineering. Smaller firms reported significantly less computer reliance.

TABLE 5.43

CORPORATE ACTIVITIES BY EXTENT OF COMPUTER RELIANCE
(Data Processing Manager Response)

	Extent of Reliance			
Corporate Activity	Totally Reliant (%)	Significantly Reliant (%)	Somewhat Reliant (%)	Not Significantly Reliant (%)
Financial and accounting data*	49.6	45.5	4.9	0.0
Personnel	6.7	28.0	33.5	31.9
Operations*	16.7	44.4	29.4	9.5
Manufacturing	5.0	23.3	37.1	34.6
Inventory	17.2	46.0	22.8	14.0
Engineering	1.1	20.2	21.3	57.4
Research and development	1.1	12.8	25.7	60.4
Planning	1.7	27.8	42.3	28.2
Other business information	2.9	34.6	43.4	19.0

*Statistically significant differences at the .05 level were found when companies were classified by size.

Major Computer Users

In assessing other aspects of company practice, data processing managers were asked to indicate major users of computerized systems in their companies for the past (1975-81), present (1982-83), and future (1984-89). Table 5.44 presents the average percentages listed by respondents. Because of inconsistent responses, these numbers do not total 100 percent. The "Other" category included such applications as operations, planning and customer branch services. While the data forecasts a reduction of computer resources devoted to finance and accounting over time, the data are inconsistent in that concomitant increases in other areas are not reflected. Reasons for this are not clear from the data.

TABLE 5.44

MAJOR USERS OF COMPUTERIZED SYSTEMS BY TIME PERIOD
(Data Processing Manager Response)

	Time Period		
	Past	Present	Future
Users	(%)	(%)	(%)
Finance	21.3	17.1	16.0
Accounting	43.3	34.4	27.3
Engineering	11.7	12.7	14.1
Inventory	13.8	13.9	14.8
Manufacturing	16.2	17.2	19.5
Distribution	18.8	17.5	16.5
General support (or corporate)	15.9	14.1	13.0
Personnel	7.2	7.2	7.4
Marketing	12.1	12.7	13.8
Other	29.1	28.1	29.8

Risk

Table 5.45 ranks the strongest internal control features. The five most important were:

1. Control measures specifically designed for our most sensitive or otherwise important control problems.

2. Formal control procedures such as separation of duties, independent reviews, reconciliations, and evaluations.

3. Quality of our personnel.

4. Company traditions and customs.

5. Attitude of top management.

TABLE 5.45

STRONGEST FEATURES OF INTERNAL CONTROL SYSTEMS BY RANK
(Data Processing Manager Response)

	Rankings				
	Strongest				Fifth Strongest
	1	2	3	4	5
Features	(%)	(%)	(%)	(%)	(%)
Control measures specifically designed for our most sensitive or otherwise important control problems	24.6	15.7	12.7	9.0	6.3
Company traditions and customs	8.2	5.6	8.6	7.8	6.7
Quality of our personnel	16.0	16.4	12.7	10.8	9.7
Attitude of top management	7.1	12.3	12.3	8.2	13.1
Monitoring of compliance with internal control measures	5.2	6.3	11.6	13.8	14.6
A widespread awareness that control measures exist	2.6	10.4	11.9	19.4	13.1
Formal control procedures such as separation of duties, independent reviews, reconciliations and evaluations	23.9	16.4	11.9	7.1	7.8
An active internal audit department	5.6	8.6	9.0	8.2	11.6

Table 5.46 provides management's assessment of potential risks associated with computerized operations in their firms. The five risks seen as potentially most serious were ranked as:

1. Testing of a recovery program in case of hardware destruction.
2. Having a recovery plan in case of hardware destruction.
3. Monitoring effectiveness and efficiency of computerized systems.
4. Not sufficiently involving internal audit with the establishment of data processing systems.
5. Ability of internal audit to audit data processing operations.

These concerns were consistent with the researchers' expectations.

TABLE 5.46

COMPUTERIZED SYSTEMS' RISKS BY EXTENT OF PROBLEM
(Data Processing Manager Response)

Risks	Extent of Problem		
	A Significant Potential Problem (%)	A Minor Problem (%)	Not A Problem (%)
Maintaining an adequate audit trail	15.8	36.8	47.4
Ability to audit actual programs	17.4	43.8	38.9
Not sufficiently involving internal audit with establishment of data processing systems	27.9	41.5	30.6
Ability of internal audit to audit data processing operations	29.6	34.6	35.8
Locating data processing personnel with sufficient expertise	22.0	45.1	33.0
Distributing data processing	21.5	32.2	46.4
Not involving operating management sufficiently with the establishment of data processing systems	20.0	46.4	33.6
Restricting access to computer information	14.3	41.4	44.4
Cost control of data processing operations	9.8	41.9	48.3
Monitoring effectiveness and efficiency of computerized systems	23.8	58.5	17.7
Transmission of computerized data via telephone or satellite	11.0	35.7	53.2
Ensuring access and security of computer facilities and backup files	19.5	36.5	44.0
Keeping backup files current	10.6	27.9	61.5
Having a recovery plan in case of hardware destruction	41.0	36.8	22.2
Testing of such a recovery program	51.5	36.0	12.5

Managers reported their firms engaged in the following:

Purchase of external computing services	62.3%
Classification of computerized data according to its sensitivity with controls instituted accordingly	71.9%
Use of microcomputers in stand-alone functions	88.4%

These areas were not, however, judged to present significant risks to internal control.

Data processing managers ranked the potential computer problems that would be the most disastrous for their organizations. Results appear in Table 5.47. The two seen to be the greatest problems were: (1) the complete or partial interruption of business activities and (2) the destruction of accounting and control records. The most frequently listed "Other" potential problem was complete destruction of the data centre due to a disaster such as fire or flood. When companies were classified by industry, utilities and petroleum and energy firms reversed the order of the two worst potential computer problems.

TABLE 5.47

**RANKING OF COMPUTERIZED SYSTEMS' DISASTERS BY
IMPORTANCE OF PROBLEM
(Data Processing Manager Response)**

	Importance of Problem				
Potential Disasters	**Most Problematic (%)**	**Second (%)**	**Third (%)**	**Fourth (%)**	**Fifth Most Problematic (%)**
Complete or partial interruption of business activities	56.3	18.3	9.0	4.9	8.2
Destruction of accounting and control records	20.9	33.2	20.1	10.1	9.3
Material inaccuracies in accounting and control records	6.7	20.1	31.0	28.7	7.5
Manipulation of accounting and control records to cover or effect irregularities	6.7	11.9	22.0	30.6	19.0
Exposure of sensitive corporate information	5.2	11.6	11.9	17.5	45.1
Other	2.2	0.4	0.0	0.0	0.4

Internal Control and External Auditor

When data processing managers were asked for their perceptions of their company's external auditors, most said they were generally satisfied with the external auditor's ability to audit computer operations (67.9 percent). Those who were dissatisfied gave the following reasons:

- External audit of computer operations is too superficial.
- No computer work performed.
- Lack of EDP expertise.
- Not thorough, consists only of a questionnaire.
- We wrote the programs they use for audit.
- Too textbook oriented.
- Auditor tends to address easy subjects and avoid difficult ones.
- Would like more audit of total systems processes as opposed to pieces.

Footnotes

[1] For a detailed discussion of analysis of variance and the distinction between one-way and two-way analyses, see Kerlinger (1973, pp. 220-266 and 271-283) and Snedecor and Cochran (1967, pp. 258-377).

Chapter 6

QUESTIONNAIRE RESULTS PART II: COMPARISONS ACROSS MANAGERIAL GROUPS AND COUNTRIES

This chapter reports on questionnaire data comparing responses where two or three levels were surveyed by common questions. It looks at how the different managers established, monitored and reported internal control practices, allowing for differences of duties, reporting responsibilities, organization and perspective to be identified.

In addition to performing one-way and two-way analyses of variance, a statistical technique used in this chapter was the Scheffe test, a multiple comparison procedure to determine where the significant differences lie after a significant F value is obtained from an analysis of variance. The Scheffe test was used to identify pairwise groups significantly different at the .10 level.[1]

Also calculated were Spearman rank-order correlation coefficients and Kendall's rank-order correlation coefficients,[2] both tests of ordinal rankings used to compare the rankings given by the different managers. The purpose of these two tests is to measure the degree of association between the two sets of rankings of the same variables. Both coefficients have a range of possible values from −1.00 to +1.00 with a high positive value indicating close agreement on the rankings given by different managers.

Objectives of Internal Control

Closely allied to definitions of internal control are internal control objectives. The objectives of an internal control system are listed in rank order of importance by the two different management levels in Table 6.1.

TABLE 6.1

RANKING INTERNAL CONTROL OBJECTIVES BY IMPORTANCE

Chief Financial Officer Rank Order	Objectives	Internal Audit Manager Rank Order
1	Safeguarding of assets	1
2	Ensuring reliability of accounting records	2
3	Prevention and detection of error	3
4	Prevention and detection of fraud	6
5	Ensuring orderly and efficient conduct of business	5
6	Ensuring compliance with management policies	4
7	Profitability and minimization of costs	7
8	Assuring effective use of company resources	8
9	Discharging statutory responsibilities to owners	9
10	Timely preparation of financial statements	10

The two levels of management were in almost unanimous agreement on their ranking of objectives. Kendall's correlation coefficient, indicating agreement in rankings, was .87. Despite management's expansion of the definition of internal control to include "managerial" aspects, it is clear that they would be in substantial agreement with their external auditors about the traditional concerns of internal control as being the most important internal control objectives.

The specific activities within CFOs' and internal audit managers' companies for which adequate internal control was most important are presented in Table 6.2.

TABLE 6.2

RANKING OF INTERNAL CONTROL ACTIVITIES BY IMPORTANCE

Chief Financial Officer Rank Order	Activity	Internal Audit Manager Rank Order
1	Cash disbursements	1
2	Cash receipts	3
3	Processing of computerized data	2
4	Purchasing	5
5	Inventory and materials handling	4
6	Payroll	7
7	Sales	6
8	International operations	8
9	Commissions, royalties or other variable payments	10
10	Other	9

It is interesting to note that the importance of processing computerized data was noted by both management levels, with CFOs ranking it third and internal audit managers second most important. Other rankings differed by only a minor degree. The Kendall correlation coefficient was .87, showing close agreement. These ranked internal control activities would also be considered important by external auditors.

Organization Structure and Internal Control

When examining internal control in Canadian corporations, it is important to understand how it is controlled by the organization, how it is monitored and how companies inform employees of internal control practices and of their own responsibilities. A number of questionnaire items were intended to examine organization structure and to determine the various management levels that contribute to the efficient operation of internal control within top Canadian corporations.

Companies acknowledging the existence of a control system by referring to it in policy letters, management statements, delegation of authority and job description are reported by the three management levels in Table 6.3.

TABLE 6.3

EXISTENCE OF INTERNAL CONTROL SYSTEM AS ACKNOWLEDGED BY MANAGERIAL GROUP

| | Reporting Officer | | |
	Chief Financial Officer (%)	Internal Audit Manager (%)	Data Processing Manager (%)
Extent			
Extensive	56.8	51.5	31.2
To some extent	42.1	45.8	62.7
Not at all	1.2	2.6	6.1

The response of data processing managers is interesting in that it differs significantly from that of the other management levels. This is further clarified by information on the extent to which company control systems were described in their company manuals. Responses are indicated in Table 6.4.

TABLE 6.4

DESCRIPTION OF CONTROL SYSTEMS IN COMPANY MANUALS

| | Reporting Manager | | |
	Chief Financial Officer (%)	Internal Audit Manager (%)	Data Processing Manager (%)
Description			
Complete	9.5	6.6	8.3
Almost complete	39.3	24.8	18.6
Partial	37.8	41.2	36.7
Very little	12.6	25.7	33.3

A one-way analysis of variance was performed, finding differences between managerial groups highly significant at the .0000 level. When the Scheffe test was applied at the .10 level, it confirmed that CFO responses were significantly different from both the internal audit responses and data processing manager responses. This statistical analysis indicated that, at the upper management levels, there was substantially more confidence in company manuals for defining internal control systems than there was at the lower levels. The data processing question was worded a little differently, asking about the internal control system of their own department only. Data processing managers, who can be expected to have a different perspective of internal control systems, apparently do not think that internal controls for the data processing departments were described to the same degree. Significant differences by company size were also found, with smaller companies describing their control systems in company manuals significantly less often (.05 level).

Companies clearly stating responsibilities of different positions and levels of authority in company manuals were estimated to be 71.7 percent by CFOs and 65 percent by internal audit.

For informing employees of company objectives, data on different management perspectives are shown in Table 6.5.

TABLE 6.5

EXTENT OF INFORMING COMPANY EMPLOYEES BY MANAGERIAL LEVEL

Information	Managerial Level		
	Chief Financial Officers (%)	Internal Audit Managers (%)	Data Processing Managers (%)
Company objectives:			
Officers and key employees	92.0	86.2	82.5
Other employees	59.7	53.9	47.0
Their personal responsibilities:			
Officers and key employees	90.9	85.8	81.0
Other employees*	83.7	76.7	74.6
Applicable internal control measures:			
Officers and key employees*	82.1	70.7	70.9
Other employees*	69.6	56.5	59.7

These data again provide evidence suggesting that the further down in the organizational hierarchy, the less the assurance that everything is well run.

Statistically significant differences by management level (ranging from .002 to .01 level) were identified for every item, first using a one-way analysis of variance, followed by the Scheffe test to identify the specific management group causing the differences. In each case, the cause of statistically significant difference was found to be the differences between the data processing managers' responses and those of the CFOs. For the last three questions [*], internal audit managers' perceptions were also significantly different from those of the CFOs.

Perspectives of differing managerial levels concerning compliance monitoring are shown by the following data:

Companies With Provision For Monitoring Compliance
With Internal Control Procedures

Chief financial officers	84.8%
Internal audit managers	81.9%
Data processing managers	69.4%

Statistically significant effects by managerial level (at the .0000 level) were identified using a one-way analysis of variance, with the Scheffe test confirming that the data processing managers' perceptions were significantly different at the .10 level from those of the other two groups.

Compliance monitoring is described in Table 6.6. Each group of managers was asked who monitored compliance with internal control procedures in their organizations.

TABLE 6.6

PROVISION OF COMPLIANCE MONITORING BY MANAGERIAL LEVEL

	Managerial Level		
Compliance Monitor	**Chief Financial Officers (%)**	**Internal Audit Managers (%)**	**Data Processing Managers (%)**
* Internal audit function	73.1	88.8	61.6
+ Controller's department	68.4	55.6	31.3
# Systems specialist	17.9	16.4	29.1
* Independent external auditors	74.9	65.5	45.9
Others	4.5	8.6	5.2

* The Scheffe test found that the data processing managers' responses were responsible for this result because of differences from CFOs' responses.
+ The Scheffe test found data processing managers' responses differed from those of internal audit.
# Internal audit and CFOs' responses were significantly different from those of data processing.

Again, a one-way analysis of variance indicated that each set of the above responses showed statistically significant differences by managerial level (from .0000 to .04).

From their perspective, data processing assessed the other three groups as providing compliance monitoring of internal control significantly less often, and data processing as providing it significantly more often. If we assume that CFOs and internal audit managers are referring to a broader set of internal controls, it would partially explain the differences. It is also quite possible that, for data processing internal controls, the data processing managers receive less assistance than the other managers believe. It is also probable, as documented by

Mautz, et al (1983) and by this study's interview results, that the other two management levels fail to understand sufficiently the internal control of management information systems.

Reporting on internal control to various parts of the organization was assessed by CFOs and internal audit managers and reported in Table 6.7.

TABLE 6.7

REPORTING RESPONSIBILITIES BY REPORTING LEVEL

	Levels Reported To					
	Financial Management		**Senior Management**		**Board or Audit Committee**	
Who Reports	CFO%	IA%	CFO%	IA%	CFO%	IA%
CEO	19.1	21.4	33.6	30.1	77.1	67.0
CFO	29.2	31.9	57.1	56.3	66.8	56.9
Controller	67.7	66.7	52.8	58.7	20.5	25.3
Internal audit	73.6	83.4	66.5	88.1	53.3	65.3
External audit	60.1	69.3	54.7	76.0	71.9	76.0
Line manager	51.5	58.2	36.6	49.4	4.0	10.1

The major difference was found in whether internal audit reports on internal control to senior management. CFOs thought that internal auditors reported less frequently than internal auditors stated they reported. This could possibly be procedural because internal audit reports could be forwarded through the CFO, causing internal auditors to see themselves as reporting to senior management, whereas CFOs saw themselves as presenting the same reports to senior management.

Those seen as primarily responsible for reporting on internal control to financial management were, in descending rank order:

1. Internal audit.
2. Controller.
3. External audit.

For major responsibility in reporting on internal control to senior management, the rank order was:

1. Internal audit.
2. External audit.
3. CFO and controller.

For reporting on internal control to the board or audit committee, the most important were:

1. Chief executive officer.
2. External audit.

Budgetary Controls

When looking at company control of expenditures, the items most frequently controlled by budgets were, in rank order:

1. Operating expenditures.
2. Capital expenditures.

More than half of all respondents agreed on this. Specific areas most frequently controlled by budgets were:

1. Contracts to sell or provide a service.
2. Inventory purchases.

Between 40 and 45 percent of executives, however, reported inventory purchases as not being controlled by budget. Although it was common to have varied levels of participation in budgetary activities, fewer than half of the divisional management reviewed the master budget. The board was the most active group in reviewing the master budget, including a post-performance review, but it participated in the budget-setting process in only a few companies.

Companies making a cost-benefit analysis before introducing significant changes in internal control are analyzed in Table 6.8.

TABLE 6.8

EXTENT OF COST-BENEFIT ANALYSIS BY MANAGERIAL LEVEL

| | Reporting Manager | | |
	Chief Financial Officers (%)	Internal Audit Managers (%)	Data Processing Managers (%)
Formal analysis	22.2	14.6	26.3
Informal analysis	65.0	72.1	58.4
No analysis	12.8	13.2	15.3

While managers differed in their perceptions of the degree of formality, it is of interest that data processing managers, in their "No analysis" response, again appeared to see fewer controls than did the other managers.

Other questions dealing with organizational structure, budget practices, corporate codes of conduct and the US FCPA are reported in the chief financial officer section of Chapter 5. Other organizational issues are also reported in the internal audit manager and data processing manager sections of Chapter 5.

The Role of Internal Audit

Since internal audit has been viewed as an integral part of most corporations' internal control systems, a large number of questions were devoted to assessing internal audit's role. Although most of these responses are reported in the earlier internal audit section of Chapter 5, some data were collected on two or all three questionnaires. Of the total, 80.1 percent of the companies had audit committees. The mining companies had the most — 100 percent — and manufacturing had the least. Forestry ranked a little below the overall average. Additional data on corporate characteristics are reported in Table 6.9.

TABLE 6.9

COMPANY STRUCTURE CHARACTERISTICS

	Reporting Manager	
	Chief Financial Officers	Internal Audit Managers
Average number of internal audit staff	10.94	9.38
Median number of internal audit staff	4.89	4.38
Companies with audit committees	79.5%	84.6%
Companies with audit committee members who were company employees	29.5%	34.1%
Companies providing organizational independence for internal audit	78.4%	78.9%
Companies providing access to board or audit committee without prior approval	72.9%	69.3%

Clearly, because only companies with an internal audit function had a manager who could respond to the internal audit manager questionnaire, it was expected that a somewhat higher percentage of internal audit managers would report that their companies had audit committees. It may also be reasonable to assume that a corporation having an internal audit function would be somewhat more likely to also have established an audit committee. The number of companies having company employees on their audit committees was, however, significantly greater than hypothesized. Control theory would suggest that this may be a questionable practice.

The percentages of industries having company employees on the audit committee are shown in Table 6.10.

TABLE 6.10

INDUSTRY PERCENTAGES FOR COMPANIES WITH EMPLOYEES ON AUDIT COMMITTEES

	(%)
Forestry	60.0
Retailing	50.0
Transportation	50.0
Petroleum and energy	38.9
Manufacturing	35.2
Mining	33.3
Financial	25.0
Utilities	11.1

Reasons for the variations shown in Table 6.10 are not clear from the data.

It is interesting that a greater percentage of the internal audit managers than of the CFOs reported having areas of the firm not open to internal audit. Percentages were: CFOs, 11.9 percent, and internal audit, 17.9 percent. Most commonly listed areas were executive payroll, head office decisions and, in some instances, general payroll. Reasons for the large discrepancy could not be determined from the data.

Those believing that internal audit now receives more emphasis than previously were in the majority. They were: CFOs, 52.3 percent, and internal audit, 65.8 percent. A likely reason for the discrepancy is the commonly noted psychological phenomenon of a particular sub-group perceiving its own function to be more important than others would perceive it to be.

Respondents were in agreement that internal audit's major role is that of consultant rather than policeman. Perceptions are presented below in Table 6.11.

TABLE 6.11

PERCEPTIONS OF INTERNAL AUDIT

Perception	Reporting Manager	
	Internal Audit Managers (%)	Data Processing Managers (%)
Seen as consultant	74.6	62.3
Seen as policeman	61.6	39.2
Seen as spy for top management		6.0
Satisfaction with above perception	60.3	N.A.

The data indicate that, perhaps, internal auditors are more sensitive to their dual role than they need to be. While surveying additional auditee groups could possibly produce different results, it appears that there may be significantly less suspicion of internal auditors within their firms than internal auditors have supposed.

Evaluating Internal Control Systems

Companies rated a number of aspects of their control systems in Table 6.12.

TABLE 6.12

RATING OF INTERNAL CONTROL SYSTEMS

	System								
	Internal Control System			Internal Audit System			Internal Audit of Computerized Systems		
Rating	CFO (%)	IA (%)	DP (%)	CFO (%)	IA (%)	DP (%)	CFO (%)	IA (%)	DP (%)
Excellent	18.2	12.6	8.6	13.3	9.2	5.8	4.5	1.9	5.5
Approaching excellence	19.8	17.1	17.1	22.9	28.6	9.9	14.0	13.4	10.6
Satisfactory	58.5	63.5	57.6	44.2	50.2	58.7	52.5	43.1	44.7
Needs major improvement	3.1	6.3	16.0	14.6	9.7	23.6	26.0	37.0	37.9

A one-way analysis of variance found highly significant differences between assessments of the different systems, as well as between managerial levels. The F probability levels were .0000 for both internal control and internal audit systems and .04 for internal audit of computerized systems. The Scheffe test indicated, for internal control systems, that the CFO group means differed significantly from internal audit means and data processing means, as did internal audit from data processing. For internal audit systems, the internal audit and CFO group means differ significantly from the data processing means. In assessment of internal audit of computerized systems, CFO responses were significantly different from internal audit responses as identified by the Scheffe test.

The data again indicate that data processing managers tend to view internal control with less confidence than other managers do. Their confidence was lowest when dealing with internal control in their area of greatest expertise — their own department. We also see, again, that lower levels in the organization have less confidence in the excellence of internal control systems than their counterparts in higher levels. Inconsistency of internal control throughout their companies was identified by 59.6 percent of CFOs, 57.6 percent of internal audit managers and 54.2 percent of data processing managers.

Executives finding company characteristics making internal control unusually difficult to maintain at an adequate level were:

Chief financial officers	35.0%
Internal audit managers	48.3%
Data processing managers	41.5%

Differences were found to be significant at the .003 level by a one-way analysis of variance. CFO and data processing responses differed significantly at the .10 level as identified by the Scheffe test.

Again, the chief financial officer was found to exhibit less overall concern over his company's internal control system than did other levels of management surveyed. Table 6.13 demonstrates the top five reasons why internal control could prove difficult.

TABLE 6.13

RANKING OF COMPANY CHARACTERISTICS
MAKING INTERNAL CONTROL DIFFICULT

	Managerial Level		
Characteristic	Chief Financial Officers	Internal Audit Managers	Data Processing Managers
Decentralization	1	2	2
Geographic dispersion	2	1	1
Need for local management autonomy	3	3	4
Small staff size	4	4	3
Diversity of business segments	5		
Rapid growth of company or industry		5	5

Despite differences in percentages of managers concerned about internal control, the preceding data indicate substantial agreement about the most important organizational characteristics contributing to difficulty in maintaining adequate internal control. The CFOs' total rankings were correlated with those of internal audit using the Spearman rank-order correlation coefficient, which was found to be .83. Correlations of CFOs and internal audit with data processing were less, at .40 and .47 respectively.

Turning to positive aspects, respondents ranked the five strongest features of their companies' internal control systems as shown in Table 6.14.

TABLE 6.14

RANKING OF STRONGEST FEATURES OF CONTROL

Feature	Managerial Level		
	Chief Financial Officers	Internal Audit Managers	Data Processing Managers
Control measures designed for most sensitive or important control problems	3	2	1
Formal control procedures	1	1	2
Quality of personnel	4	4	3
Company traditions and customs			4
Attitude of top management	2	3 (tied)	5
Widespread awareness that control measures exist	5		
Active internal audit department		3 (tied)	

Again, there are only minor differences in identification of the most important controls. Close relationships were further shown by the Spearman rank-order correlation coefficient indicating .92 agreement between CFOs and internal audit, .74 between CFO and data processing, and .52 between internal audit and data processing. Data processing ranked "attitude of top management" as somewhat less important, possibly because this department may receive less direct supervision from top management. Lack of widespread computer expertise among top management could also have been a contributing factor.

Internal Control Risks

Risk factors were directly assessed by all managers using two specific questions, in addition to questions addressed specifically to the individual levels. When asked which company activities caused the greatest concern, responses were as shown in Table 6.15.

TABLE 6.15

RANKING OF INTERNAL CONTROL RISKS

	Managerial Level	
Risk	**Chief Financial Officers**	**Internal Audit Managers**
Electronic data processing	1	1
Inventory, receiving, shipping and materials handling	2	2
New or greatly expanding company operations		3
Product pricing	4	
Decentralized operations	3	5
Purchasing	5	4

Again, concerns appeared substantially the same with the Spearman rank-order correlation coefficient being .84. The CFO perspective on purchasing confirms other interview results expressing similar concerns. For electronic data processing and purchasing, regulated companies showed significantly more concern than nonregulated companies (.05 level). Regulated companies reported significantly more concern (.05 level) about financing, external financial reporting, inventories, investments, and new or expanding company operations. The other question assessing risk directly addressed computerized operations. Results are presented in the following section.

Internal Control and Computerization

Because respondents identified electronic data processing as the company activity causing the most concern from an internal control perspective, it is of some interest to note what the greatest potential risks of computerized operations themselves were perceived to be. These results are shown in Table 6.16.

TABLE 6.16

RANKING OF RISKS OF COMPUTERIZED OPERATIONS BY MANAGERIAL LEVEL

	Managerial Level		
Risk	**Chief Financial Officers**	**Internal Audit Managers**	**Data Processing Managers**
Monitoring effectiveness and efficiency of computerized systems	1	3	3
Maintaining an adequate audit trail	2	1	
Ability to audit the actual programs	3	4	
Having a recovery plan in case of hardware destruction	3	5	2
Testing such a recovery plan	4	2	1
Ability of internal audit to audit data processing operations			5
Not sufficiently involving internal audit with the establishment of data processing systems			4

One-way analyses of variance indicated a statistically significant difference (.05 level) for all items ranked except for "Having a recovery plan. . . ." It had been hypothesized, however, that data processing managers would see the issues of audit trails and of auditing the programs in use as less important than would incumbents of the other two positions. For overall ranking order, the Spearman rank-order correlation coefficient indicated a correlation of .90 for CFOs and internal audit, and .83 for CFO and data processing ranking.

Unregulated companies reported significantly more concern over computerized systems risks than regulated companies did at the .05 level for the following: ability of internal audit to audit data processing, cost control of data processing, monitoring data processing effectiveness and efficiency, and transmission of computerized data over telegraph or telephone facilities.

Data were collected from several questions concerning the organization of data processing within the company structure.

Companies providing training in data processing for company managers not familiar with it were reported by CFOs as 61.5 percent and by data processing managers as 46.8 percent. Those differences need not be entirely caused by differences in perspective; some could be explained by managers receiving data processing training outside the company.

There was agreement on whether companies were providing for a search for new computer applications to protect the company's competitive advantage. Reporting affirmatively were 67.6 percent of CFOs and 67.4 percent of data processing managers.

Companies with a budget for such activities were a considerably lower proportion. CFOs were 41.8 percent, and data processing managers, 36.4 percent.

A potential problem was found, also identified in Mautz, et al. (1983), in that companies providing for advancement opportunities within the company for the chief information officer were reported as: CFOs, 52.3 percent and data processing managers, 31.6 percent. An obvious discrepancy existed concerning advancement opportunities for data processing managers, who apparently viewed their advancement opportunities as more restricted or less defined than CFOs viewed them.

A charge-back system for data processing costs existed in 59.9 percent of CFO respondents' firms and 57.3 percent of data processing respondents' companies. In the majority of instances, it was a full-cost, charge-back system. The systems were generally designed to control data processing costs. Managers agreed that data processing specialists were found as internal audit team members in less than half of the companies. The responses were: internal audit managers, 47.1 percent and data processing managers, 47.2 percent. Data processing managers reported, however, that their personnel were seconded to act as technical consultants to internal audit in 90.7 percent of cases and that almost 70 percent had coordinating committees for computerized systems.

Firms classifying computerized data according to its sensitivity and instituting controls accordingly were in the majority. Responses were internal audit managers, 68.2 percent and data processing managers, 71.9 percent.

Questions about responsibility levels for computerized operations were asked on all three questionnaires, with results shown in Table 6.17.

TABLE 6.17

PRIMARY AND OTHER RESPONSIBILITY LEVELS
FOR COMPUTERIZED OPERATIONS

Responsibility	Level Responsible +
Assigning responsibility for computerized systems	1. CFO 2. Data processing manager Other: Line manager
Responsibility for acquisition of computerized systems	1. Data processing manager
Cost control over development and operations	1. Data processing manager Other: CFO
Measuring efficiency and effectiveness of computerized systems	1. Data processing manager Other: CFO and line manager
Assuring reliable computer security	1. Data processing manager Other: CFO
Audit of data processing activities	1. Internal audit manager
Design of computerized systems	1. Data processing manager Other: Line manager
Sign-offs of computerized systems	1. Data processing manager 2. CFO*
Integrity of operating data	1. Data processing manager 2. Line manager Other: CFO
Assuring adequate controls built into computerized data	1. Data processing manager 2. CFO
Authorizing changes to computerized systems	1. Data processing manager 2. Line manager

+ Primary responsibilities are indicated by 1, or 1 and 2 where data indicated divergence of practice. "Other" levels are also indicated, where these appeared to be used by a substantial number of companies.
* These two responses were very close.

Data processing managers saw themselves as the group primarily responsible for computerized systems in virtually every instance except sign-offs of computerized systems. For sign-offs, they saw line management as being most responsible, while the others, particularly the CFOs, saw data processing as primarily responsible for sign-offs.

When asked to whom they reported on internal control, data processing managers most frequently stated that they reported to the CFO. Those receiving data processing managers' reports are indicated below as:

Chief financial officer	51.1%
Chief executive officer	13.1%
Controller	12.7%
Others	24.3%

Managers were questioned about whom they reported to on internal control. Table 6.18 shows these results.

TABLE 6.18

REPORTS BY MANAGERIAL LEVEL

	Managerial Level		
Reporting To:	**Chief Financial Officers (%)**	**Internal Audit Managers (%)**	**Data Processing Managers (%)**
Senior management			74.6
Chief executive officer	27.5	35.9	
Chief financial officer	52.7	66.9	
Controller	35.4	41.3	
Internal audit	19.8	23.8	24.6
External audit	11.8	8.9	20.5
Line manager	35.6	39.2	
Other			4.9

Even in reporting the "Other" category, data processing managers did not mention that line managers received their reports. This perception may be due to someone else in the organization forwarding these reports. It may also be concluded that the data processing managers referred to the CEO and CFO as senior management, because this reported percentage is similar to those reported by the CFOs and internal audit managers.

Perceptions of External Auditor

Data on organizational satisfaction with external auditors were collected from all managers. Results appear in Table 6.19.

TABLE 6.19

SATISFACTION WITH EXTERNAL AUDIT BY MANAGERIAL LEVEL

	Managerial Level		
Activity	**Chief Financial Officers (%)**	**Internal Audit Managers (%)**	**Data Processing Managers (%)**
Audit of financial information	97.3	89.7	
Audit of computerized operations	79.7	49.6	67.9

There appears to be a high level of satisfaction with traditional audit activities, but less with audit of computerized operations. A one-way analysis of variance found statistically significant differences between groups at the .0000 significance level for the latter.

Canadian and US Internal Control Comparisons

One purpose of this study was to examine similarities and differences between Canadian and US internal control environments. Using studies by Mautz et al (1980, 1981 and 1983) as bases for the US information, comparisons are presented where US data permit. The Mautz study (1980) detailed many internal control practices of a procedural nature, such as charts of accounts and bank reconciliations, that were not researched in this study. In the later US studies (1981 and 1983), the coverage of topics such as control of computerized systems was undertaken using interviews and seminar discussions, allowing for only general comparisons between the more extensive Canadian data and the information provided by the earlier US studies. Another substantial difference is that the US study surveyed only chief financial officers. Nevertheless, questions with the same intent were asked of Canadian and US managers, making some numerical comparisons possible. The comparisons follow. Rank-order correlations were not performed because, in some instances, wording differed, or the same questions were not asked of both sets of CFOs.

Canadian and US CFO Comparisons
One similarity that became apparent during the interview stage of this study was that the two groups had similar definitions of internal control. Neither Canadian nor US managers were willing to distinguish between the accounting controls and the administrative controls that external auditors have emphasized (Mautz and Winjum, 1981).

The existence of a control system was recognized more extensively according to Canadian chief executive officers (56.8 percent) than by their US counterparts (39.4 percent) (Mautz, et al., 1980, p. 17). Table 6.20 shows that the percentages indicating comprehensive efforts made to convey internal control practices to employees were almost identical.

TABLE 6.20

**COMMUNICATION OF INTERNAL CONTROL INFORMATION
BY EMPLOYEE CATEGORY**

| | Employee Category | | | |
| | Officers and Key Employees | | Others | |
Information	Canadian (%)	US (%)	Canadian (%)	US (%)
Company objectives	92.0	92.3	59.7	54.8
Their personal responsibilities	90.9	92.0	83.7	81.1
Applicable internal control measures	82.1	77.3	69.6	57.3

US companies reported having a written code of conduct 75.3 percent of the time (Mautz, et al., 1980, p. 23), with Canadian companies reporting a lower statistic at 63.5 percent. Where codes of conduct existed, companies in both the United States and Canada made an effort to ensure that officers and key employees received copies of the code. US companies required that employees sign for conformity with the code of conduct more frequently than Canadian companies did.

	Canadian	US
Officers and key employees	71.3%	86.5%
Other employees	20.3%	28.7%

Firms in both countries provided for disciplinary actions for those violating the code, with Canadian companies making this provision in 65 percent of cases and, in the United States, in 63.5 percent of cases. The code was enforced in 72.4 percent of Canadian companies and in 61.3 percent of US companies.

As might be expected, the areas of budgets and control over expenditures were similar in Canadian and US companies. Where approval was required for groups to exceed specified amounts, there were basically no differences between the levels required by Canadian and US firms. The levels primarily required were senior officers, senior management or the full board (Mautz, et al., 1980, p. 25).

A formal cost-benefit analysis was undertaken more frequently in the United States when a company was introducing significant internal control changes. Canadian companies undertook a formal analysis in 22.2 percent of the cases, while US firms made a formal analysis in 34 percent of cases.

The Role of Internal Audit

As was expected, there were significant differences in the size of internal audit departments reported for Canada and the United States. Canadian audit departments had an average size of approximately 11; in the United States the average size was 25. The staff size ranged in Canada from 1 to 99 and, in the United States, from 1 to 1,000. Additional data are presented in Table 6.21. While sizes of departments varied greatly, the percentage of companies having an internal audit department was similar.

TABLE 6.21

ASPECTS OF INTERNAL AUDIT BY COUNTRY

	Country	
	Canada (%)	US (%)
Companies with internal audit departments	80.1	87.5
Chief internal auditor provided with organizational independence	78.4	66.6
Internal audit has access to board or corporate audit committee	72.9	77.6
Areas of the firm where internal audit is denied access	11.9	7.4

The most notable difference shown in Table 6.21 is the organizational independence of the chief internal auditor, with independence lower in the United States than in Canada. This may be somewhat offset by the access internal audit has to the board and corporate audit committee and by the fact that fewer areas are restricted from internal audit in the United States. Areas where internal audit was denied access included salaries, head office records and executive salaries in both Canada and the US (Mautz, et al., 1980, p. 17).

Table 6.22 shows how managers rated their internal control systems.

TABLE 6.22

RATING OF INTERNAL CONTROL SYSTEM BY COUNTRY

	Internal Control System	
Rating	**Canada (%)**	**US (%)**
Excellent — includes all measures that can be justified	18.2	5.8
Approaching excellence — final improvements are either in process of implementation or under consideration	19.8	19.4
Satisfactory — needs minor improvement	58.5	65.4
Needs major improvement	3.1	6.7

US chief financial officers were more critical, rating their systems as excellent less frequently. A few more noted that their systems required improvement than did Canadian CFOs (Mautz, et al., 1980, p. 38).

US companies provided for monitoring of procedures more frequently than did the Canadian firms, with 96 percent and 84.8 percent, respectively, reporting this provision. Compliance monitoring was assessed as shown in Table 6.23.

TABLE 6.23

COMPLIANCE MONITORING BY COUNTRY

	Country	
Rating:	**Canada (%)**	**US (%)**
Excessive	0.8	0.3
About right	76.4	70.1
Less than desirable	14.4	28.8
Compliance monitoring provided by:		
Internal audit function	73.1	95.7
Controller's department	68.4	88.7
Systems specialist	17.9	44.3
Independent external auditors	74.9	87.2
Others	4.5	14.4

US companies appeared to be less satisfied with their own compliance monitoring than Canadian companies were. A somewhat higher degree of interdependence in compliance monitoring was shown for US companies. The list of "Others" in both samples included the CFO, line management reviews and the use of outside consultants.

US CFOs reported more inconsistent quality of internal control throughout their companies (72 percent) than did Canadian CFOs (59.6 percent). As shown in Table 6.24, the reasons offered for this inconsistency were similar, though not identical.

TABLE 6.24

RANKING OF REASONS FOR INCONSISTENCY OF INTERNAL CONTROL

Canadian Rank	Reason	US Rank
1	Characteristics of a specific division or unit	–
2	Characteristics of a division's or unit's staff	–
3	Lack of management attention	3
–	Permitted variations in management style	1
–	Geographical dispersion	2

The reasons listed as first and second by Canadian CFOs were listed under "Others" by their US counterparts.

Certain company characteristics were thought to make internal control unusually difficult in 35 percent of the Canadian companies and in 32 percent of the US companies (Mautz, et al., 1980, pp. 43-44). The top three reasons are shown in Table 6.25.

TABLE 6.25

RANKING BY COUNTRY OF CHARACTERISTICS MAKING INTERNAL CONTROL DIFFICULT

Canadian Rank	Characteristic	US Rank
1	Decentralization	1
2	Geographic dispersion	2
3	Need for local management autonomy	4
6	Rapid growth of company or industry	3

Canadian and US companies indicated a different distribution of areas where adequate internal control was thought most important as shown in Table 6.26.

TABLE 6.26

RANKING OF ACTIVITIES MOST IMPORTANT TO CONTROL

Canadian Rank	Activity	US Rank
1	Cash disbursements	1
2	Cash receipts	4
3	Processing of computerized data	(not asked)
4	Purchasing	3
5	Inventory and materials handling	2
6	Payroll	5
7	Sales	6
8	International operations	7
9	Commissions, royalties, or other variable payments	9
10	Other	8

The three strongest features of CFOs' companies are presented in Table 6.27.

TABLE 6.27

RANKING BY COUNTRY OF STRONGEST FEATURES OF INTERNAL CONTROL SYSTEMS

Canadian Rank	Feature	US Rank
1	Formal control procedures such as separation of duties, independent reviews, reconciliations and evaluations	6*
2	Attitude of top management	1
3	Control measures specifically designed for our most sensitive or otherwise important control measures	2
4	Quality of personnel	3

*Worded slightly differently in the US study.

Canadian managers ranked formal control procedures as more important than US CFOs did.

The area of internal control causing most concern in both Canada and the United States was the risk associated with computerized information systems. The second area of risk in Canada was inventory, which appeared on the US list most often under "Other." Decentralized operations and purchasing were also identified as major risk areas in both samples.

Canadian-US Comparison of Internal Audit and Data Processing
Comparisons between the role of the internal audit manager and the data processing manager in the two countries are outlined in this section. Included in

the data processing discussion will be aspects of computerized information systems within the organization.

In the 1980 US study, internal audit managers and data processing managers were interviewed but not surveyed. The resulting US data are, therefore, based on a total of 49 individuals, while the Canadian statistics are based on a sample of 232. Comparisons should be viewed in light of this discrepancy.

In Canada, internal auditors reported that their role was viewed by others as being a policing role in 61.6 percent of cases. This compared to 25 percent in the US. In both countries, however, the main role was viewed as a dual one of policeman and consultant.

The incidence of having an EDP audit specialist within the internal audit department was lower in Canada than in the United States. The US percentage was 57.1 while the Canadian one was 47.1. Of the 49 internal audit managers interviewed in the United States, 22 stated that they had two or more EDP auditors, six had only one EDP auditor and 21 did not have any EDP audit specialists.

The external auditors were said to rely on internal audit's work in both the United States (89.7 percent) (Mautz, et al., 1980, p. 114) and in Canada (83.1 percent). This was said to decrease audit fees in a majority of both Canadian and US companies.

Data processing managers in both countries were not totally satisfied with the ability of external auditors to audit computerized information systems (Mautz, et al., 1980, p. 151). Reasons given were primarily that external auditors did not have the expertise nor the time to audit these systems properly. This dissatisfaction, then, is widespread.

The role of internal audit was viewed rather negatively by US data processing managers (Mautz, et al., 1980, pp. 39-40). While this question was not asked directly of the Canadian data processing managers, it was noted that the majority of Canadian managers thought of internal audit as a consultant function and, in their written comments, Canadian data processing managers were primarily supportive of their internal audit departments.

For evaluation of data processing, the feedback of operating departments, meeting their budgets and developing of new applications were very important in Canada. US firms reflected the same attempts to provide user satisfaction (Mautz, et al., 1980, p. 62).

Managers in both countries ranked the same potential computer disasters as most ominous: the complete or partial interruption of business activities and destruction of accounting records.

In general, the studies identified more similarities than differences in internal control problems, risks, organizational structure and internal control in general as practised by the largest corporations in North America.

Footnotes

[1] The Scheffe test and its relationship to analysis of variance is described in Kerlinger (1973, pp. 234-238).

[2] Spearman rank-order correlation coefficients and Kendall rank-order correlation coefficients are very similar tests of ordinal rankings. For a more in-depth description of these tests, see Siegel (1956, pp. 202-223).

Chapter 7

SUMMARY AND CONCLUSIONS

A major contribution of this study is the provision of a large data bank that enables analysis and depiction of the state of internal control in the largest Canadian corporations. The study covered a broad area; it identified and investigated internal control practices found in companies. The findings of this study should provide a basis for future research. The extensive data collected should contribute to an understanding of how internal control within corporations is established and maintained. Another contribution is that the study enables an intra-organizational perspective of internal control to be developed encompassing four levels of managerial responsibility.

While details of the findings have been presented in Chapters 5 and 6, this section of the report focusses on main conclusions, presenting them in summary form. Main trends and practices in these top companies were quite identifiable, but it should be noted that there is great diversity of practice. For every issue investigated, some corporate executives reported that their companies did it differently; that they used a variety of practices different from those identified as being most widely used.

An important contributing factor was the cooperation of Canadian business leaders, resulting in a particularly favourable response rate. Their willingness to assist in this project demonstrates their deep interest in a topic found to be important by all management levels.

RESPONDENTS' DEFINITION OF INTERNAL CONTROL

The managers involved in this research gave broad interpretations of internal control. Because external auditors' definitions were readily available, one study objective was to determine whether inside management viewed internal control to be composed of similar elements. In their definitions, Canadian managers agreed substantially with a definition formulated by the Financial Executives Institute Canada (1981), which extended internal control:

> . . . beyond specific procedures undertaken in the accounting, financial and audit functions . . . the internal control system includes many other factors, such as management philosophy, organization structure, quality of personnel, delegation of responsibility, with commensurate authority and segregation of duties (p. 5).

The managers agreed that internal control included accounting controls and management controls. Accounting controls were defined as those applying to accounting data and financial controls. Management controls referred broadly to management policies, efficiency and effectiveness, and value for money, including such aspects as performance review. They displayed considerable reluctance to distinguish between preventive and detective controls, stating that those were linked together and that defining them separately did not really contribute to the practice of internal control in their companies.

Objectives of Internal Control

Knowing the objectives management intends to achieve in establishing the company's internal control systems assists in understanding corporate practice. The implications are that top priority will be given to the objectives found most important and that major checks and balances and compliance testing will be devised around those priority controls. It is also of interest to determine which of management's objectives overlap with those of concern to external auditors.

In examining what the Canadian business sector may understand internal control to be, the major objectives of internal control as defined in the literature and by managers themselves can be classified as either financial and accounting control objectives or management control objectives. Using such a classification, we observe that managers in the study ranked them as follows:

Rank Order	Financial and Accounting Control Objectives	Rank Order	Management Control Objectives
1	Safeguarding of assets	4	Prevention and detection of fraud
2	Ensuring reliability of accounting records	5	Ensuring orderly and efficient conduct of business
3	Prevention and detection of error	6	Ensuring compliance with management policies
9	Discharging statutory responsibilities to owners	7	Profitability and minimization of costs
10	Timely preparation of financial statements	8	Assuring effective use of company resources

When specific company activities and transactions were considered, the subjects again placed heavy emphasis on transactions and activities that have traditionally been the purview of accountants, such as cash disbursements, cash receipts, purchasing and inventory. Most of these have traditionally also been examined thoroughly by outside auditors. That management's three most important objectives were financial accounting objectives, and that areas traditionally the responsibilities of accountants were rated as most important to control is evidence of a continuing strong degree of congruity of interest between company management and the public accounting profession. A company's auditors could be seen to be performing a function for management beyond the attest function for financial statements when they provide an impartial assessment of these important financial accounting controls. It should also be noted that the role of the company's internal audit department was seen as an increasingly important one in a company's monitoring of its business activities.

THE ORGANIZATION OF INTERNAL CONTROL

Establishing goals and objectives for internal control systems and specifying the components of the systems are important management activities. A concomitant requirement is that these specifications must be conveyed to managers and the roles of the various participants assigned. Following such communication, definition of reporting relationships and a system for monitoring of internal control procedures is required.

The Audit Committee

One significant organizational component of internal control is the audit committee. This study found that the proportion of Canadian companies having audit committees (80 percent) was virtually unchanged from that reported in a 1981 CICA study. In 1981, the number of firms having company officers or former officers serving on the audit committee was reported to be 47 percent of companies surveyed (44 percent of the largest 300 companies). This more extensive study found company officers on the audit committee in approximately 30 percent of the sample. The trend, therefore, appears to be away from using company officers on the audit committee. No statistically significant differences by size of company were found in this data for companies either having audit committees or having company members on the audit committee.

Assigning Responsibility

In the specification of company control systems, through policy statements, job descriptions, delegation of authority, etc., data processing managers assessed their companies favourably in this regard less frequently than did CFOs and internal audit managers. They also reported their companies as providing less description of their control systems in company manuals than did the other managerial levels. As expected, smaller companies described their systems in company manuals less frequently. Data processing managers also reported that fewer officers and company employees were informed of company objectives, personal responsibilities and applicable internal control measures although, for the latter, internal audit and data processing managers agreed that there was less information conveyed than the CFOs believed. It is evident that internal control of data processing activities is less clearly defined in these companies than internal control of other areas. It is also evident that more CFOs believed that all groups were more fully aware of both their personal responsibilities and internal control measures than the other managers did.

There was additional evidence that the data processing group was less satisfied with the state of health of internal control when monitoring of compliance with internal control procedures was assessed. When responsibility for compliance monitoring was examined, internal and external audit were found to have major responsibility for data processing activities. These differences in satisfaction with compliance monitoring basically conformed to prior expectations.

In designing internal control systems, approving the system, evaluating system effectiveness and authorizing changes to the system, responsibility was shared and distributed among various managerial levels, with more than one managerial level being responsible for each function. Design responsibility was mainly the controller's; approving the system was performed by CFOs, with CEOs also participating in a large proportion of companies. External and internal auditors were those mainly charged with evaluating system effectiveness, while authorizing systems changes was largely the responsibility of CFOs, controllers and CEOs.

Codes of Conduct

Corporate codes of conduct were found to be valuable in communicating and ensuring the cooperation of personnel in internal control practices. A similar item, judged important by a minority, was management attention. All levels of management were more satisfied with the quality of their internal control level when their superiors also viewed it as being important.

Role of Internal Audit

That internal audit is an important function in internal control in Canadian corporations was an important finding, well documented by the study results. Eighty percent of companies responding have an internal audit department, which is the same as those reporting having an audit committee. Slightly more than half of the companies used the internal audit department as a training ground for new recruits. Although this could have disadvantages to internal audit when their auditors who have just become well trained are transferred to other areas, it could also have advantages. In terms of elevating internal control consciousness and of trainees acquiring understanding of a wide range of corporate activities, the practice could be a very positive one.

An interesting finding was that, while internal audit personnel saw their organizational role as primarily that of consultants, they believed that most of the time (61 percent) they were also seen as policemen. Data processing managers, however, saw internal auditors as policemen in 39 percent of cases. If theirs was a company that rotated financial management trainees into internal audit, that too could have a favourable effect on their perceived role in other areas because a number of managers would have been former internal auditors themselves.

Overall, internal audit was well regarded in companies. The internal audit system, in general, was ranked higher than the ability of external audit to audit computerized systems and was also regarded more highly in general by interviewees.

Slightly fewer than half of the internal audit departments had a computer audit specialist, but data processing managers were drafted as advisers to internal audit in more than 90 percent of companies. That this is an adequate provision seems unlikely, because 37 percent of both internal audit and data processing managers rated internal audit of computerized systems as "needing major improvement," as did 26 percent of CFOs. Some of this minority group held quite strong opinions concerning shortcomings for this activity. Data processing managers viewed both their companies' internal control systems and internal audit systems less favourably than other managers did. This perception of less confidence in control effectiveness by data processing managers was widespread, touching many internal control practices in the firm and is one of the study's major findings.

When reporting relationships were examined, it was found that internal audit bears the major responsibility for reporting on internal control to financial and senior managements. Several levels were responsible for reporting on internal control to the board or audit committee, with CEO, CFO, external audit and internal audit all having important reporting responsibilities. About 70 percent of companies provided internal audit with access to the board or audit committee without requiring prior approval, but only 60 percent of internal audit managers stated that their audit committees received reports from internal audit. Auditees appeared to be well consulted, probably helping to support the perception of internal audit as rendering assistance.

When companies evaluated internal audit's performance, feedback from auditees was slightly more important than the judgment of the CFO, but savings achieved also rated in half the companies.

CONTROL OF COMPUTERIZED INFORMATION SYSTEMS

One of the major findings of this study is that the primary internal control problem faced by Canadian companies is the control of computer-based systems. This has been well documented in the literature and is also well documented by this study's research findings.

When ranking internal control risks, electronic data processing headed the list, with inventory, receiving, shipping and materials handling ranking second. Of computerized operations, CFOs and internal auditors saw the greatest potential risks to be maintaining an adequate audit trail and having the ability to audit the actual computer programs themselves. Also, all managers were concerned with having a recovery plan in case of hardware destruction and the testing of such a plan.

That CFO and internal audit manager concerns were shared was supported by data processing managers. They would like to increase the involvement of internal audit with the initial establishment of new data processing systems, yet believed, at the same time, that the ability of internal audit to audit data processing operations is a serious potential risk.

The problems that data processing managers thought would be most disastrous to their organizations were the complete or partial interruption of business activities and the destruction of accounting and control records. Some of those differences conform to original hypotheses and would be caused, at least in part, by the differing organizational responsibilities of the three managerial groups. That these concerns are serious is attested to by evidence about reliance on the computer for company activities. While smaller companies reported a lesser degree of computerization, computer reliance for financial and accounting data was almost complete in most companies. Only research and development and engineering activities were reported as being not significantly reliant on the computer by more than half the company respondents.

While a majority of companies declared that they provided for a search for new computer applications to protect the company's competitive advantage, not only did a significantly lower proportion of CFOs and data processing managers report having a budget for this search, but the percentage of data processing managers was lower than the CFO percentage. This could suggest that, without the indication of priority conveyed by a budget for such a search, it might not receive sufficient managerial attention. In the interviews, one manager assessed the devotion to maintaining competitive computer advantage to be "probably more form than substance." This finding was also supported by a discussion of the same issue in Mautz, et al., (1983, pp. 70-71).

To control data processing costs, a charge-back system, usually full-cost charge-back, was used by more than half of the companies. Many operating managers participated in the budgeting process for computerized information systems. Data processing performance was evaluated using a large number of criteria, supporting their perceptions of themselves as a service department. Most important among these groups and/or criteria were: feedback from operating departments; judgment of their immediate superior (which was the CFO in about one half of companies) and development of new applications. There were also a large number of other important evaluation factors, making it not surprising that 30 percent of data processing managers were dissatisfied with the way in which they and their departments were evaluated. Many of those dissatisfactions were related to what were perceived to be misconceptions surrounding data processing's role, together with lack of knowledge by other company managers.

Data processing managers were less satisfied than other managers with internal control in general and with the internal control of their operations specifically. One likely factor here is their more intimate knowledge of data processing controls, as well as their being more aware of the problems involved. Another is that, as staff specialists, they are somewhat separated from the rest of the organization. Almost 70 percent of data processing managers did not have advancement opportunities specified by the company, indicating further that, unlike internal audit, data processing managers are more isolated and may find advancement within the company difficult. Unlike US data processing managers, however, Canadian managers had considerable longevity with their firms. Perhaps the raiding of other companies for skilled EDP managers will increase in the future in Canada as computerization increases and shortages of expert personnel become more acute.

That future changes in computerization are anticipated was evidenced when only about one-fourth of managers found their hardware and software capable of meeting needs over the next five years. They found, in general, their software to be less current than their hardware. Some industries were found to face more serious problems of obsolescence than others.

All levels of managers were concerned with the ability of internal audit to audit EDP systems, but confidence in the external auditor was even lower. These findings mirror the concerns of public accounting bodies and public accounting firms. An interesting comment, which may sum up the problem from a number of perspectives, was made by one chief financial officer who stated that, in his opinion, Canadian CAs were "going on luck." He noted that "to express an opinion (about computer controls) within a good fee is difficult, and time for computer experts to assess controls is never enough."

GENERAL RISKS AND WEAKNESSES

Geographic dispersion was widely seen as one organizational factor leading to internal control risk. Other widely cited weaknesses were in the following categories: lack of an internal audit department, lack of ability to audit computerized systems, unspecified goals for computerized systems, and general lack of specification of policies and procedures. Many managers cited lack of policy as a major shortcoming of their internal control systems.

The results of this study have confirmed a classic phenomenon initially identified by Dearborn and Simon (1958) and documented repeatedly in subsequent studies of operating organizations. It is that each executive sees a problem in terms of his or her own department's function within the organization, and often weights his or her responsibility and contribution as more significant than executives from other departments would weight it. Thus, we observe CFOs reporting that they have more responsibility to top management than other levels report for them and internal audit managers reporting their department as being more important in internal control issues than other managers assess it to be. These "biases" conformed to expectation, however, and were certainly no more pronounced than those found by other researchers in other settings. Given such functional fixation, a clearer picture was developed by collecting data from more than one level within the organizations studied.

The study data and interview results demonstrated that companies within regulated industries appear to experience fewer control difficulties than those that are unregulated. The process of complying with regulatory requirements, although costly in terms of resources, apparently has some offsetting benefits in the form of improved internal control and lowered concerns about external financial reporting.

CANADIAN-US COMPARISONS

The US Foreign Corrupt Practices Act of 1977 had affected fewer than 30 percent of Canadian corporations. Within those companies, however, the positive results reported were similar to those reported by US companies. Some

consequences reported in this study as a result of the passage of the act included:
- Issuance of new policies.
- Institution of a formalized corporate code of conduct.
- Use of internal control reviews and reports.
- Additional internal audit emphasis.
- Better documentation of internal control systems.

When the Canadian internal control environment was compared to that of US corporations, more similarities than differences were found. For example, the importance of internal audit, the major risks associated with electronic data processing and most reporting relationships were much the same. Managers defined internal control in substantially the same way. Canadian companies defined their systems more specifically and were a little more satisfied with their practice of internal control. US and Canadian companies alike were concerned about external audit's ability to audit computerized information systems.

Despite the differences cited, and contrary to initial concerns, one of the major findings of this study was that US and Canadian corporate internal control practices and problems showed almost no substantial differences. It appears, therefore, that many of the conclusions of this study can be applied to internal control generically, rather than to internal control in an exclusively Canadian setting.

Chapter 8

RECOMMENDATIONS

This chapter offers some broad recommendations based on the findings of common practice within the organizations that were studied. They are also based on the shortcomings many executives noted with concern within their companies. Although the recommendations are far reaching, some companies may already have implemented some or many of them. In its application, internal control is a combination of many factors that must fit the organization, its industry and the situations in which they are applied. Managers should consider these recommendations carefully to determine whether they are applicable to their corporate environment and whether they will mesh with controls already in place.

ORGANIZATIONAL STRUCTURE

1. Authority and responsibility for internal control should be fully explained to management throughout the firm. Managers without clearly specified responsibilities, job descriptions and policy guides felt the lack keenly. Additional communication about company objectives, performance evaluation criteria and the internal control practices associated with responsibilities for various corporate activities will help to ensure that a system of "checks and balances" exists and will make performing to objectives more easily achievable.

2. Where a corporate code of conduct does not exist, the board and top management should implement one. Companies with a code of ethics find it helpful to convey top-level concern about both the appearance and the reality of the ethical climate of their company. It can serve as a communication medium and may also serve the legal purpose of defining proscribed activities.

3. Top management attitudes toward internal controls are important in determining how seriously they are viewed throughout the organization. Where compliance monitoring was undertaken, feedback was thought highly important by managers surveyed. Prompt feedback conveys top-level interest and can facilitate performance improvement.

AUDIT COMMITTEES

4. In those jurisdictions where audit committees are not mandated, the formation of audit committees is recommended for companies that do not have them at present. It is also recommended that internal audit and external audit

should be provided with access to the audit committee without top management's prior permission. The audit committee can designate a reporting structure for a contingency such as a requirement for a line manager or internal audit department to report company wrong-doing or incompetence.

5. It is suggested that companies with audit committees that have, at present, company officers serving as members should alter this policy. Although they may have complete confidence in the integrity of all committee members, the potential appearance of a conflict of interest makes such a practice inadvisable. Because many firms specifically cited the interest of a particularly diligent outside member of the audit committee, this source of outside expertise should not be overlooked in achieving good internal control.

INTERNAL AUDIT

6. The researchers strongly recommend that companies without an internal audit department establish one. The major functions of an internal audit department are: to act as a consultant; ensure that a system of internal controls is in place and operating effectively; and provide support for the external auditor. Many companies also use an internal audit posting to train management personnel. Of companies with internal audit departments, 32.2 percent had two or fewer staff and 15.9 percent reported a one-person staff. Half of the companies surveyed had four or fewer people in internal audit, therefore, the establishment of an internal audit department need not be expensive. Virtually all executives reported that, in their companies, the benefits to all levels of the organization substantially exceeded the costs.

7. The lack of follow-up procedures for the recommendations of internal audit was seen as a shortcoming by firms who did not have them. In some instances, delays of up to two years for receiving feedback on their recommendations were cited. Conversely, companies with such procedures often referred to them as a particularly positive feature of their own internal control systems. If both areas seen as requiring improvement and areas where controls are judged to be good are identified to the departments involved, motivation is enhanced, enabling departments to more readily improve their performance.

COMPUTERIZED INFORMATION SYSTEMS

8. Computerized information systems are an integral part of large Canadian business organizations. Wherever possible, it is recommended that the internal audit staff include a designated systems audit specialist. Lack of expertise in auditing EDP systems was listed repeatedly as a major shortcoming. Help from internal audit in establishing internal controls for data processing systems was not widely reported, but large numbers of data processing managers stated that such help would be highly desirable for their companies. Given the forecasted increases in computerization for a wide ranging variety of functions, such expertise should become even more important in the future than it is now.

9. Training of diverse management groups in computerized systems is also recommended. Many data processing managers thought that their function, and the constraints and problems they faced, were not well understood by others in the company. The training process will accomplish two objectives: (1) promote communication between departments and increase user awareness of data flows and the systems and (2) promote the team concept, enlisting the participation of systems specialists and systems users particularly in the development and enhancement of systems. There is also a strong possibility of cost reduction because as the "trial" phase can often be shortened if the original specifications and requests are made by line management with greater expertise.

10. Companies who wish to protect or increase their competitive advantage through the improved service and cost-saving that accompanies the effective use of computers should establish adequate budgets to search for such computer applications changes.

11. Specifying change procedure for computer systems is recommended as a promising area for control definition. Either a lack of specified systems change procedures or an over-zealous bureaucracy can lead to problems, ranging from impeding new or innovative computer systems to poor control or possible subversion of the systems. Companies with particularly good change procedures often cited this as a strong feature of their company's control environment.

12. More attention should be given to disaster recovery plans for computerized systems. The plans should include the traditional areas of alternate processing sites and facilities to continue operations, as well as the nontraditional area of estimation of potential losses for computer catastrophe.

13. It is recommended that the role of the data processing manager be defined, together with opportunities for his or her advancement. This can maintain professional motivation and can also serve to alleviate the "job-hopping" found in US companies, which could occur in Canadian firms if the only way to obtain advancement is to move to another company for a promotion and salary increase.

RISK

14. It is recommended that companies undertake a more formal examination of the costs or potential costs of internal control risks seen by their managers. Although risks identified as being widely present have been recognized in previous recommendations, there were sufficient sincere concerns expressed about corporate practice within the respondents' firms in responses to the open-ended questions and during interviews to indicate that a non-threatening company inquiry would be successful in identifying areas for investigation.

EXTERNAL AUDITORS

15. The final recommendation concerns external auditors. Although the public accounting profession is aware of the need for increasing knowledge of

computerized systems among members, these research findings document the need anew. Just as within the corporation, external auditors also need to increase their knowledge over time as the computer evolution continues.

We conclude this study with the hope that the study findings and recommendations will assist in maintaining internal control at a high level in the Canadian corporation.

Appendix A

Interview Guides*

Chief Executive Officer
Interview Guide

1. Please describe your:
   (a) Present position and length of tenure
   (b) Previous position and length of tenure
   (c) Background (education, professional designation, and experience) (Discuss generic control as a lead-in.)
2. Internal Control vs. Management Control:
   (a) What do you understand by the term "internal control"?
   (b) Do you and others in your company distinguish between accounting control, internal control and management control?
3. Control Consciousness and Environment:
   (a) Please evaluate and discuss the level of control consciousness in this company.
   (b) What causes this? (e.g., CFO's attitude, a past experience, attitude of other officers, employee morale, company policy.)
   (c) What, in your view, are the key elements of a company's internal control environment?
   (d) Do you do anything specific yourself in your capacity as a company officer to improve or strengthen the internal control environment in your company?
4. Use of Resources for Internal Control:
   (a) If you could spend 20% more for internal control purposes, how would you use it?
   (b) If you had a 20% reduction, what would you trim back?
5. Control of Divisions and Subsidiaries:
   (a) How does your company establish and monitor the internal control of divisions, wholly-owned, and less-than-wholly-owned subsidiaries?
   (b) Does dispersion, size, etc., present internal control problems?
6. Internal Control Risks:
   (a) What do you consider to be the major internal control risks faced by your company? (e.g., security of physical assets, financial assets, other; *single incident and other types.*)
   (b) Do you have other major control problems?
   (c) Are there specific characteristics of your company which make internal control particularly easy or difficult? (Please describe, e.g., structure, geography, people movement, etc.)

[* Modelled, with permission, after the interview guides found in Mautz, et al., 1980.]

(d) Have your external auditors made suggestions regarding your internal control in connection with their annual audit? Is it something that comes to your attention? Do you rely upon the CFO to take action and report the results to you? Could you give us a general idea of the auditors' suggestions?

(e) What methods do you have of monitoring other than accounting reports (e.g., efficiency of a division)?

(f) Do you feel that the recession has affected your organization's internal control?

7. Corporate Code of Conduct:

(Are you prepared to discuss this area of your organization?)

(a) Do you have an unwritten code of conduct? Who is aware of this code?

(b) Do you have a written code of corporate conduct?

(May we have a copy of your corporate code of conduct?)

How long have you had one? ＿＿＿＿＿ months. ＿＿＿＿＿ years.

(c) Who receives copies?

(d) What action is taken for a breach of conduct?

(e.g., reprimand, note in personnel record, dismissal order, what circumstances?)

(e) How many people had an action taken against them in last two years? What form of action?

8. Executive Perquisites:

(a) How are *executive perquisites* controlled? (i.e., zero interest loans, executive compensation plans, expense accounts?)

(b) Who approves your expense accounts?

9. Executive "Override":

(a) How does your company deal with "executive override"?

(b) What is to prevent any company officer from requiring employees to bypass controls? (e.g., fear of discovery, control consciousness, an "ombudsman" function, quality of people.)

10. Channels for Reporting to an Ombudsman:

(a) If an employee or junior officer felt a need to discuss a superior's conduct pertaining to internal controls or a failure to comply with company policies, is there someone to whom he could go with minimum fear of harm to himself? (e.g., audit committee, internal audit department, chairman of board, a special officer.)

(b) If "yes", have all employees been so informed?

(c) Have these channels been used?

11. US Foreign Corrupt Practices Act:

(Know if this company is a subsidiary or parent of a US corporation. Note if this is the case.)

(a) How has your firm been affected by the US FCPA?

(b) If so, what steps has your company taken to comply with the FCPA?

(c) Were these helpful, in your opinion?

(d) If this firm is not a subsidiary or parent of a US firm, then ask . . . "Are you aware of the US FCPA?"

12. Who reports on internal control/accounting control to:

(a) Financial management?

(b) Senior management?

(c) The board or audit committees?
13. What is the composition of the audit committee of your firm?
    (a) What is your philosophy about a CEO sitting on the audit committee?
    (b) Does the audit committee formally review the firm's internal controls?

May we have a copy of your firm's most recent financial statements?

Chief Financial Officer
Interview Guide

1. Please describe your:
   (a) Present position and length of tenure
   (b) Previous position and length of tenure
   (c) Background (education, professional designation, and experience)
       (Discuss generic control as a lead-in.)
2. Internal Control vs. Management Control:
   (a) What do you understand by the term "internal control"?
   (b) Do you and others in your company distinguish between accounting control, internal control and management control?
3. Control Consciousness and Environment:
   (a) Please evaluate and discuss the level of control consciousness in this company.
   (b) What causes this? (e.g., CEO's attitude, a past experience, attitude of other officers, employee morale, company policy.)
   (c) What, in your view, are the key elements of a company's internal control environment?
   (d) Do you do anything specific yourself in your capacity as a company officer to improve or strengthen the internal control environment in your company?
4. Use of Resources for Internal Control:
   (a) If you could spend 20% more for internal control purposes, how would you use it?
   (b) If you had a 20% reduction, what would you trim back?
5. Control of Divisions and Subsidiaries:
   (a) How does your company establish and monitor the internal control of divisions, wholly-owned, and less-than-wholly-owned subsidiaries?
   (b) Does dispersion, size, etc., present internal control problems?
6. Internal Control Risks:
   (a) What do you consider to be the major internal control risks faced by your company? (e.g., security of physical assets, financial assets, other; *single incident and other types.)*
   (b) Do you have other major control problems?
   (c) Are there specific characteristics of your company which make internal control particularly easy or difficult? (Please describe, e.g., structure, geography, people movement, etc.)

(d) Have your external auditors made suggestions regarding your internal control in connection with their annual audit? Is it something that comes to your attention? Do you rely upon your staff to take action and report the results to you? Could you give us a general idea of the auditors' suggestions?

(e) What methods do you have of monitoring other than accounting reports (e.g., efficiency of a division)?

(f) Do you feel that the recession has affected your organization's internal control?

7. Corporate Code of Conduct:
(Are you prepared to discuss this area of your organization?)

(a) Do you have an unwritten code of conduct? Who is aware of this code?

(b) Do you have a written code of corporate conduct?
(May we have a copy of your corporate code of conduct?)
How long have you had one? _____ months. _____ years.

(c) Who receives copies?

(d) What action is taken for a breach of conduct?
(e.g., reprimand, note in personnel record, dismissal order, what circumstances?)

(e) How many people had an action taken against them in last two years? What form action?

8. Executive Perquisites:
(a) How are *executive perquisites* controlled? (i.e., zero interest loans, executive compensation plans, expense accounts?)

(b) Who approves your expense accounts?

9. Executive "Override":
(a) How does your company deal with "executive override"?

(b) What is to prevent any company officer from requiring employees to bypass controls? (e.g., fear of discovery, control consciousness, an "ombudsman" function, quality of people.)

10. Channels for Reporting to an Ombudsman:
(a) If an employee or junior officer felt a need to discuss a superior's conduct pertaining to internal controls or a failure to comply with company policies, is there someone to whom he could go with minimum fear of harm to himself? (e.g., audit committee, internal audit department, chairman of board, a special officer.)

(b) If "yes", have all employees been so informed?

(c) Have these channels been used?

11. US Foreign Corrupt Practices Act:
(Know if this company is a subsidiary or parent of a US corporation. Note if this is the case.)

(a) How has your firm been affected by the US FCPA?

(b) If so, what steps has your company taken to comply with the FCPA?

(c) Were these helpful, in your opinion?

(d) If this firm is not a subsidiary or parent of a US firm, then ask . . . "Are you aware of the US FCPA?"

12. Who reports on internal control/accounting control to:
(a) Financial management?

(b) Senior management?

(c) The board or audit committee?

13. What is the composition of the audit committee of your firm?
    (a) What is your philosophy about a CEO (or a CFO) sitting on the audit committee?
    (b) Does the audit committee formally review the firm's internal controls?

    May we have a copy of your firm's most recent financial statements?

Chief Internal Auditor
Interview Guide

A. Background

1. Please describe your:
   (a) Present position and length of tenure
   (b) Previous position and length of tenure
   (c) Major responsibilities
   (d) Background (education, experience and professional affiliations)
2. How does internal audit fit into the organizational structure?
   How is internal audit independent of those it audits?
   (If possible, obtain organizational chart.)
   (a) Describe frequency and nature of reporting on internal audit activities to your *immediate* superiors.
   (b) Who else receives these reports?
   (c) What action is taken upon receipt? (e.g., Acknowledge receipt only. Used in evaluating internal audit performance. Internal audit is called upon to elaborate on findings.)
   (d) Who (besides external auditors) reviews audit programs?
   (e) Has the audit committee reviewed internal control? Were you present at this meeting?
3. How often are you called upon by the following groups to perform an activity on their behalf? What is the nature of that activity? What do they do with the findings?
   (a) Board of directors/audit committee.
   (b) Chief executive officer.
   (c) Financial VP
   (d) Controller.
   (e) Operating managers (e.g., division head, plant manager).
   (f) EDP and other support functions.
4. Organization of audit function
   (a) How is the internal audit function organized? (e.g., centralized? decentralized?)
   (b) Are there internal audit activities carried out by personnel who do not report to you? Please describe (e.g., division auditors, outside consultants/examiners).

5. Relationship with external auditor
   (a) Do external auditors review the internal audit program? (May have answered in question A.2.)
   (b) What specific tasks do external auditors request of internal audit? (e.g., evaluation and tests of internal control.)
   (c) Are external audit fees lower because of the work that internal audit does for the external auditors? How much? (e.g., now 50% of what they would be without internal audit's assistance.)
   (d) (How) Is the relationship with external auditors changing with the change from manual systems to EDP?
6. Please describe the size and composition of internal audit professional staff.
   (a) Total personnel?
       (1) Accounting trained?
       (2) Nonaccounting trained?
   (b) EDP auditors?
       (1) From accounting background?
   (c) Operational auditors?
       Major changes in the size and composition of internal audit staff?
       (1) Over past 5-10 years?
       (2) Over next 5-10 years?
   (d) What is your budget?
   (e) Are adequate resources allocated to internal staff?
       (1) Where would/could you use more personnel? (Cost/benefit justified?)
       (2) Where would/could you use fewer personnel? (Cost/benefit justified?)
7. Evaluation of internal audit
   (a) How is internal audit evaluated?
   (b) What specific actions have resulted from this evaluation in the recent past (5 years)? Please describe.
   (c) How, in general, are internal auditors evaluated?
   (d) Who are your peers with respect to internal auditing? How well does your internal audit group rate with respect to your peers? (e.g., rate well in comparison with other internal audit groups in same industry.)

B. Internal Control

The purpose of this section is to determine your view of internal controls in your company.
1. In your opinion, what is the relationship between internal audit and internal control?
2. What do you view as the greatest exposure in your company in terms of internal control?
   (a) What is the single worst incident of "breakdown" in internal control that you can envision?
   (b) What major areas of gradual control erosion can you envision?

   (c) What has been done/could be done to minimize the probability or effect of that occurrence?
3. In your opinion, are formal/informal controls uniformly applied?
   (a) In all locations? If not, please describe how controls vary. (e.g., foreign remote, small, joint ventures, partly owned subsidiaries.)
   (b) To all types of projects or activities? (e.g., R&D, nonroutine activities.) If not, please describe how controls vary.
4. In general, (how) are controls changing in your company? (e.g., scope, formality.)
   (a) In response to the US Foreign Corrupt Practices Act?
   (b) For other reasons?
5. What is your overall evaluation of controls in your company? (e.g., in comparison to other companies with which you are familiar.)
6. In your opinion, what (if anything) could be done to improve the controls of activities in your company? (e.g., documentation, formalization, personnel training.)
7. Who reports on internal control/accounting control to:
   (a) Financial management?
   (b) Senior management?
   (c) The board or audit committees?

C. Internal Audit's Role and Activities

1. Audit initiation.
   (a) What percentage of internal audit resources are used for:
       (1) Routine (e.g., recurring) audits _____
       (2) Special audits _____
   (b) Who initiates:
       (1) Routine audits? _____
       (2) Special audits? _____
2. Using an example of a typical audit, please describe the audit process from the point at which the auditee was selected to the disposition of the findings.
   (a) How are auditees selected? (e.g., organizational units vs. activities? Dollar size? Randomly selected sizes? Exposure to risk?)
   (b) Frequency of audits?
   (c) Auditee's view of internal audit? (Consulting vs. policing function? Internal audit is the "eyes and ears of management/directors/external auditors"?)
   (d) Auditee's input to auditors report?
   (e) Disposition of findings? (Action taken? Follow-up?)
3. Are there any activities or parts of the organization which are off-limits to internal audit? (e.g., executive payroll; minutes of *all* meetings; executives' activities.)
4. Please indicate how much of internal audit's resources are directed toward auditing each of the following:
   (Definition of terms is important. Obtaining precise percentage's is unimportant.)
   (a) Management's objectives for internal control as per the *Handbook:*

    (1) Discharge of statutory responsibilities, for example
maintaining accountability to owners. _____%
    (2) Profitability and minimization of costs. _____%
    (3) Prevention and detection of fraud and errors. _____%
    (4) Safeguarding of assets. _____%
    (5) Reliability of accounting records. _____%
    (6) Timely preparation of reliable financial information. _____%
  (b) Other audit activities:
    (7) Operational efficiency and effectiveness. _____%
    (8) Adherence to other organizational policy (e.g.,
payroll, code of conduct). _____%
    (9) Compliance with external regulations other than
GAAP (e.g., FCPA, FIRA, Revenue Canada). _____%
   (10) Other (please describe) _____

_____

_____ Total _____%

  (c) Please indicate your definition of "asset" as used in this context.

5. Internal audit's view of internal auditing.

  (a) What do *you* see as the purpose and role of internal audit in the organization? (e.g., consultant vs. policeman; operational vs. financial; preventive vs. detective.)

  (b) Changing role and activities of internal auditing:

    (1) (How) Has internal audit's role and activities changed over the past several years?

    (2) What (if any) changes do you foresee in the future?

    (3) What are the causes of those changes? (e.g., management style, external accountability.)

6. What is (are) the most significant (positive or negative) finding(s) by internal audit in the past year?

7. Auditing EDP

  (a) What has been the history of the involvement of internal audit in development and operation of EDP systems? (Always been involved; originally not involved but now there are X EDP auditors; involved in operation but not in development; are active members of the EDP steering committee.)

  (b) How and when does internal audit get involved in the design, implementation and operation of a data processing system? (Feasibility, design, implementation, test operation.)

  (c) How do you ensure the auditability of data processing systems?

Data Processing Manager
Interview Guide

A. Data Processing Environment

1. Please describe your:

  (a) Present position and length of tenure.

  (b) Previous position and length of tenure.

  (c) Background (education and experience).

2. How does data processing fit into the organization's structure?
   (a) To whom do you report?
       President/CEO
       Vice President of Finance, Engineering, _____
       Comptroller
   (b) Who are the users of DP services?
       Accounting   _____%
       Engineering   _____%
       Manufacturing   _____%
       _____   _____%
       _____   _____%
   (c) Has the current usage and/or reporting structure evolved in the last few years, and/or you see it changing in the next few years? (i.e., how have minicomputers, microcomputers, online processing, database management, or distributed processing impacted this company? Has there been a major shift in usage patterns?)
   (d) Does each division have its own DP operation? What control over divisional DP does corporate DP have and how is the control exercised?

3. Data processing environment?
   (a) Hardware Environment
       i. Computer: large machines
                    medium
                    mini computers
          If more than one,
              Are they geographically distributed?
              Are they interconnected?
              If yes, what purpose (remote job entry, data sharing, processor sharing)?
       ii. Computer terminals
           Approximate number
           Type (keyboard printer, CRT, graphics, microcomputers, intelligent)

4. Data Processing Budget
   What is your annual budget?   _____
   Approximate distribution among:
     Personnel   _____
     Hardware (purchase, rental, maintenance)   _____
     All other   _____
   Do you feel the resources allocated to data processing are adequate?
   If your budget was increased by 20%, what would you do with it?
   _____% Hardware (main memory, processor, secondary storage terminals)
   _____% New Software (database management, teleprocessing application development)
   _____% Personnel (hiring, training, salary increases)
   _____% Current Software (maintenance, documentation, auditing)
   _____% Other

5. Use of service bureaus:
   (a) What outside data processing services does your company use? (service bureaus, time sharing vendors, keying services, special printing services, etc.)
   (b) What potentially sensitive programs or data do you make available to the outside supplier?
   (c) What measures are taken to ensure the safeguarding and accuracy of these resources?

B. Computerized Data Files

1. Data files
   What is the approximate number of major data files on your system? (e.g., customer, inventory)   _____
   What is the approximate number of minor data files on your system? (e.g., daily transactions, program library   _____
   What is the average size of − a major data file?   _____
   (In million characters)
                          − a minor data file?   _____
2. Data sharing
   Is there much data sharing between
   i. Application areas (e.g., both accounts receivable and order processing are concerned with customer records). Is the sharing concurrent?
   ii. Multiple users of a single application (e.g., several order processing clerks may wish to access the customer file). Is the sharing concurrent?
   If you have interactive programs, do they *update* master files online? (or do they submit online changes for later processing?)
3. Data control
   How finely is access to the computer's data files controlled? (The list below is progressively tighter control; "a" or "c" are most usual.)
   (a) use of the computer system
   (b) use of a specific program
   (c) opening of specific data file
   (d) processing of a transaction type
   (e) access to specific data fields in a file
   (f) access to specific records in a file
   (g) access to specific data fields in a specific record
4. Personnel
   With respect to data management, there are four support roles that data processing might play:
   i. Maintaining data quality (editing of both new or existing data)
   ii. Facilitating data access (providing a menu of available data and assisting users in getting to it)
   iii. Controlling data access (establishing and verifying authorization for data access)
   iv. Guarding against data loss (providing backup and recovery procedures) Is there a specific individual or group of individuals who fill these roles?

Individuals	Number	Role Filled			
		i.	ii.	iii.	iv.
Data Entry Supervisors Librarians "Senior" Analyst(s) Database Administrator(s) Other: _____					

Which of these functions do you feel are most important?
Which of these functions do you feel are performed most effectively?

C. Involvement With Internal Audit:

1. What data processing systems either provide a large amount of internal control and/or, if improperly built, maintained, or used, could lead to the largest misuse of corporate resources? (This question is a discussion vehicle for those that follow.) (e.g., inventory control system could provide an effective means for accounting for and safeguarding physical assets or it could be a vehicle for improper use of resources.)

2. (a) What has been the history of the involvement of internal audit in development and operation of EDP systems?
   (Always been involved; originally not involved but now there are X EDP auditors; involved in operation but not in development; are active members of the EDP steering committees.)

   (b) When, and how, and why did the environment change if ever? (New manager of internal audit; major breach of internal control in an EDP system; a specific new major system development brought the issue to the forefront?)

3. (a) What is your view of the internal audit group?
   (Viewed as another user of major systems; assists in the responsibility for adequate internal control facilities of systems; wish they would be more/less involved in EDP systems.)

   (b) Are they very suspicious and cautious? Do they understand DP technology? (Active or passive involvement; consultant or reviewer; do they help or hinder?)

4. Who is responsible for internal control in EDP systems?
   (User, DP, auditors.) (If there is an internal control problem, who is to blame?)

5. Does the company use a formal methodology for controlling the design and implementation of EDP systems?
   (Developed by the company; purchased from a consulting company. Name of methodology?)

6. (a) What is the role of internal audit in the design and implementation activities. (Advisory, active, sign-off?)

(b) If active involvement, when and how does internal audit get involved in the design and implementation of systems? (e.g., perform a formal review of the design proposed before implementation begins and/or must sign-off on a system, along with the user, before the system is placed in operation.)

7. Might user pressure to get a system up quickly (often) result in a reduction in the number of internal controls you build into the system? In the control of the system development itself?
   (Controls are only installed when there is time; if the user needs the system in a hurry, we bypass the internal audit review.)

8. Does internal audit actually review and/or sign-off on *all* EDP systems? Might the small size or short life expectancy or experimental nature, or importance or special purpose of the user group exempt a system from review:
   (Only financial systems are reviewed; only operational and control (not planning) systems are reviewed; engineering systems are not reviewed.)

9. How are existing EDP systems selected for audit and what procedures are used to audit them?
   (a) How selected? Politically sensitive, cheque writing, amount resources managed, liquidity of resources, user complaints, frequent changes.
   (b) How is the audit performed? Formal documented procedure; computer tools; documentation of results.

10. How many members of the internal audit staff audit EDP systems? Is this enough, too little, too many? What is their background and training?
    (a) Does internal audit have enough resources to keep up with new and changing systems? How many EDP auditors should there be?
    (b) Where do EDP auditors come from? Where do they go?

11. Are data processing personnel (analysts, programmers, and operators) trained in and motivated by internal control considerations?
    (a) Who is trained?
    (b) How are they trained? (Formal, informal)

D. Features of the EDP Control System

1. Controls over access:
   (a) How is physical security of the computer hardware, terminal areas, telecommunication lines, and file libraries maintained?
       (e.g., locks, guards, keys, entry register, locked vaults)
       (b) Describe your operating system controls on a system sign-on, program execution, file access, file update. (Account number, password, terminal location, time of day, etc.)

2. Control over program changes:
   (a) What is the procedure for entering or modifying programs in the library? (How easy would it be to make an unauthorized change in the accounts receivable or accounts payable program?)
   (b) How does internal audit track changes in programs once they are operational? (From your experience is a modified program very likely to be audited; how long before the change is audited?)

3. Backup and Recovery Plans:
   (a) Describe the controls over your data files.
       (1) Frequency of backup copies?
       (2) Location of backup storage?
       (3) Disposition of transaction files?
       (4) Typical example of data loss?
       (5) Average time till recovery?
       (6) Are you very comfortable with the current system?
   (b) Describe the backup and recovery program of the computer facilities. (e.g., What if there is a fire in the computer?)
       (1) Is there a documented plan?
       (2) How and when is it tested?
       (3) Does it rely on backup facilities internal or external to the company?
       (4) Has the plan been independently reviewed?
4. What is the role of the external audit in the auditing of EDP systems?
   (a) What does the external auditor do? (Procedure, frequency, resource usage.)
5. Internal Control Aspects of EDP:
   (a) How do you compare the internal control aspects of EDP in your company with others in your industry?
   (b) What is the major weakness in the internal control aspects of your EDP environment?
       (1) If there was an industry/peer group standard, how would you rate?
       (2) What is the most current concern? Is it company or industry specific?
6. If someone in a position of trust wanted to:
   (a) sabotage equipment
   (b) remove the accounts receivable file
   (c) remove a copy of your customer files
   (d) read sensitive information from the personnel file (salary)
   (e) modify the accounts payable file
   (f) modify the accounts receivable program; how difficult would it really be? How about for:

	a	b	c	d	e	f
Senior analyst						
Junior programmer						
Manufacturers' customer engineer						
Internal auditor						
External auditor						
A visiting consultant						

Probably could: ✔
Impossible: x
Don't know: blank

Appendix B

COVER LETTERS AND QUESTIONNAIRES

Canadian Institute of
Chartered Accountants,
150 Bloor Street West,
Toronto, Ontario
M5S 2Y2

Society of Management
Accountants of Canada,
154 Main Street East,
Hamilton, Ontario
L8N 3C3

October 31, 1983

Internal Control In Canadian Corporations

The Canadian Institute of Chartered Accountants and The Society of Management Accountants of Canada are jointly sponsoring a study to find out how Canadian management views the control systems installed in their corporations.

The research is designed to gather information about the practices employed to develop and establish control systems in Canadian corporations. To gather the required information, researchers Dr. L.D. Etherington and Dr. I.M. Gordon have developed three separate questionnaires -- one for the Chief Financial Officer, one for the Internal Audit Manager and one for the Data Processing Manager. **In order to reflect the appropriate viewpoint please complete the questionnaire yourself. Also, please complete it independently of the other two respondents.**

Questionnaires were developed with a group of business practitioners whose input was provided to ensure that the study be of as much value as possible to management. Mr. Kenneth H. Smith, President of the Financial Executive Institute Canada has also endorsed this research by stating:

"It is particularly gratifying that the focus will be on the management perspective as opposed to the external perspective and I am most impressed with the description of the objectives, scope and methodology. Accordingly I feel confident that the results of the study will be of sound, practical value to senior business management...I would encourage the prospective respondents to this study to give their fullest cooperation".

We are requesting your cooperation in this first examination of Canadian internal control practices. This research is intended to determine actual Canadian practice and not to present an idealized version of internal control. You will be making a significant contribution to its success if you just "tell it like it is".

R.D. Thomas, FCA
General Director of Research
Canadian Institute of
Chartered Accoutants

D.P. Armishaw, MBA, RIA
Director of Research
Society of Management
Accountants of Canada

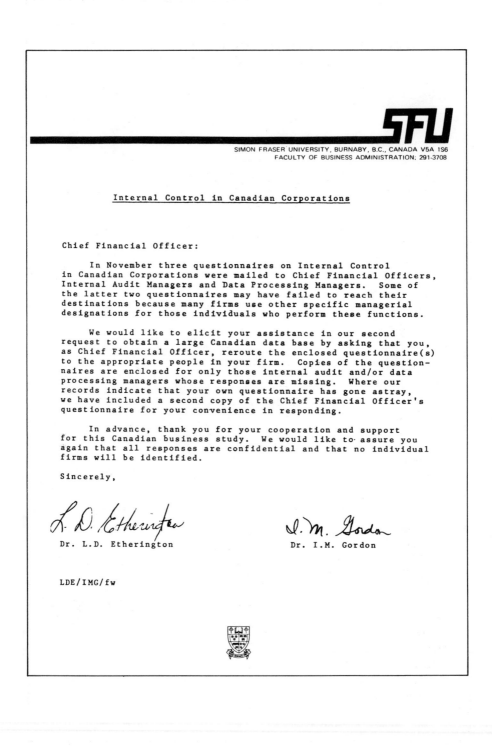

SFU

SIMON FRASER UNIVERSITY, BURNABY, B.C., CANADA V5A 1S6
FACULTY OF BUSINESS ADMINISTRATION; 291-3708

<u>Internal Control in Canadian Corporations</u>

Chief Financial Officer:

In November three questionnaires on Internal Control in Canadian Corporations were mailed to Chief Financial Officers, Internal Audit Managers and Data Processing Managers. Some of the latter two questionnaires may have failed to reach their destinations because many firms use other specific managerial designations for those individuals who perform these functions.

We would like to elicit your assistance in our second request to obtain a large Canadian data base by asking that you, as Chief Financial Officer, reroute the enclosed questionnaire(s) to the appropriate people in your firm. Copies of the questionnaires are enclosed for only those internal audit and/or data processing managers whose responses are missing. Where our records indicate that your own questionnaire has gone astray, we have included a second copy of the Chief Financial Officer's questionnaire for your convenience in responding.

In advance, thank you for your cooperation and support for this Canadian business study. We would like to assure you again that all responses are confidential and that no individual firms will be identified.

Sincerely,

Dr. L.D. Etherington

Dr. I.M. Gordon

LDE/IMG/fw

RESEARCH PROJECT ON INTERNAL CONTROL IN CANADIAN CORPORATIONS

sponsored jointly by

CANADIAN INSTITUTE OF CHARTERED ACCOUNTANTS	AND	SOCIETY OF MANAGEMENT ACCOUNTANTS OF CANADA

CHIEF FINANCIAL OFFICER QUESTIONNAIRE

INTRODUCTION

The emphasis of this study is upon internal control from management's perspective. The objectives of the study are to: explore management's understanding of internal control, to examine how it is practiced in top Canadian corporations, to identify risk factors, and to determine who is responsible for various aspects. This will also be the first Canadian study to conduct an empirical examination of the role played by computerized information systems in internal control of the large corporation, and to assess risks created by this new technology. It is anticipated that the findings of this study should substantially assist Canadian companies in assessing their own internal control practices.

As is customary for such studies, all information obtained will be treated as *confidential* and will be used only in tabulated summaries without company identification of any kind. Questionnaires, the identity of respondents, and specific responses will be available only to members of the research team.

With very few exceptions, the questions can be answered by placing a check mark or a rating number in one of the boxes provided. Please read the question completely before beginning to answer.

Please return within ten days to:
Dr. L.D. Etherington
Dr. I.M. Gordon
Faculty of Business Administration
Simon Fraser University
Burnaby, B.C.
V5A 1S6

Demographic Data:

Sex ☐ ☐
Male Female 7

	Yes	No	
Academic Degree	☐	☐	8

If yes, please specify _____ 9-14

	Yes	No	
Professional Designation	☐	☐	15

If yes, please specify _____ 16-21

Industry Information:

Industry:
Retailing ☐ Transportation ☐
Manufacturing ☐ Forestry ☐ 22
Mining ☐ Utilities ☐
Petrol. & Energy ☐ Financial Services ☐
Other ☐

(Please specify) _____ 23-24

Size of firm within ☐ ☐ ☐ 25
your industry: Large Medium Small

Are you within a Yes No
regulated industry? ☐ ☐ 26

PART I

These questions are intended to discover the extent of the internal control practices now employed within your company.

Question No. 1

To what extent does your company acknowledge the existence of a control system by referring to it in policy letters, management statements, delegation of authority and job description?

☐ ☐ ☐
Extensively To some extent Not at all 27

Question No. 2

Check the boxes indicating the organizational level(s) at which the following occur:

	Designs Internal Control System	Approves the System	Evaluates System Effectiveness	Authorizes Changes to the System	
Chief Financial Officer	☐	☐	☐	☐	28-31
Controller or Chief Accounting Officer	☐	☐	☐	☐	32-35
Internal Audit Manager	☐	☐	☐	☐	36-39
Chief Executive Officer	☐	☐	☐	☐	40-43
External Auditor	☐	☐	☐	☐	44-47
Audit Committee or Board	☐	☐	☐	☐	48-51

Question No. 3

Is a comprehensive effort made to inform officers and employees of:

	Officer and Key employees		Other employees		
	Yes	No	Yes	No	
Company objectives?	☐	☐	☐	☐	52-53
Their personal responsibilities?	☐	☐	☐	☐	54-55
Applicable internal control measures?	☐	☐	☐	☐	56-57

Question No. 4

Please indicate your perception of the importance of the following objectives of a system of internal control:

	Very Important	Somewhat Important	Of Little Importance	Not Important	
Prevention and detection of fraud.	☐	☐	☐	☐	58
Prevention and detection of error.	☐	☐	☐	☐	59
Ensuring orderly and efficient conduct of business.	☐	☐	☐	☐	60
Discharging statutory responsibilities to owners.	☐	☐	☐	☐	61
Safeguarding of assets.	☐	☐	☐	☐	62
Profitability and minimization of costs.	☐	☐	☐	☐	63
Assuring effective use of company resources.	☐	☐	☐	☐	64
Ensuring reliability of accounting records.	☐	☐	☐	☐	65
Timely preparation of financial statements.	☐	☐	☐	☐	66
Ensuring compliance with management policies.	☐	☐	☐	☐	67
Other (please specify)	☐	☐	☐	☐	68
_____					69-70

Question No. 5

To what extent is your internal control system described in company manuals? (Please check the appropriate box.)

Completely	☐	Partially	☐	6
Almost completely	☐	Very little	☐	
Other (please explain)	☐			
_____				7-8

	Yes	No	
Are responsibilites of different positions and levels of authority clearly stated in company manuals or instructions?	☐	☐	9

Question No. 6

Check the boxes indicating the organizational level(s) at which the following occur:

	Reports on Internal Control to Financial Management	Reports on Internal Control to Senior Management	Reports on Internal Control to Board or Audit Committee	Receves Data Processing Manager's Report	
Chief Exec. Officer	☐	☐	☐	☐	10-13
Chief Finan. Officer	☐	☐	☐	☐	14-17
Controller	☐	☐	☐	☐	18-21
Internal Audit	☐	☐	☐	☐	22-25
External Audit	☐	☐	☐	☐	26-29
Line Manager	☐	☐	☐	☐	30-33

Question No. 7

	Yes	No	
Does your company have a written code of corporate conduct?	☐	☐	34
Who receives a copy?			
Officers and key employees?	☐	☐	35
Other employees?	☐	☐	36
Who signs periodically for conformity with code?			
Officers and key employees?	☐	☐	37
Other employees?	☐	☐	38
Do procedures exist for discipline of those violating the code?	☐	☐	39
Have disciplinary measures ever been enforced?	☐	☐	40
Is there a designated person to whom an employee could report bypassing of company policy or internal controls?	☐	☐	41

What other ways could this come to light? (Please specify)

_____	42-43
_____	44-45
_____	46-47

Question No. 8

This question refers to budget practices.

Indicate by check marks in the appropriate boxes the organizational level(s) at which the following occur:

	Unit or Department Management	Divisional Management	Corporate Management	Board of Directors	
Participation in the budget setting process	☐	☐	☐	☐	48-51
Reviews the master budget	☐	☐	☐	☐	52-55
Compares actual results with budgeted results	☐	☐	☐	☐	56-59
Reviews explanations of documented material differences.	☐	☐	☐	☐	60-63

Question No. 9

Indicate (a) the extent to which each type of expenditure listed below is or is not restricted as to amount in the normal course of business, and (b) the level of approval required (such as independent senior officer, committee of directors, or full Board) to exceed the imposed limit, if any.

	(a) Nature of Limit			(b) Level of Approval Required to Exceed Limit	
	None	Budgeted Amount	Fixed Maximum Amount		
Operating expenditures	☐	☐	☐	_____	64,65-66
Inventory purchases	☐	☐	☐	_____	67,68-69
Capital expenditures	☐	☐	☐	_____	70,71-72
Incurrence of debt: Under one year	☐	☐	☐	_____	73,74-75
More than one year	☐	☐	☐	_____	6,7-8
Contracts to sell or provide service	☐	☐	☐	_____	9,10-11

Question No. 10

	Formal Analysis	Informal Analysis	No Analysis	
Does your company make a cost benefit analysis before introducing significant changes in internal control?	☐	☐	☐	12

Question No. 11

	Yes	No	
Are you required to comply with the U.S. Foreign Corrupt Practices Act?	☐	☐	13

If you have taken any actions to comply with	14-15
this act, please identify_____	
_____	16-17
_____	
_____	18-19
_____	20-21

Does your industry have particular internal control problems you are wrestling with? (Please specify)	22-23
_____	
_____	
_____	24-25

When your last major internal control improvement was made, who was responsible for the idea? (Please indicate)	26-27
_____	28-29

Question No. 12

This question refers to internal audit and the Audit Committee.

	Yes	No	
Does the company have an internal audit function?	☐	☐	30
How large a staff? _____			31-32
Does the chief internal auditor have organizational independence (i.e., not dependent for job, pay, or promotion purposes) from those responsible for the activities audited?	☐	☐	33
Do you have an audit committee?	☐	☐	34
Does the internal audit function have access to the Board of Directors or the Corporate Audit Committee without requiring approval from any company officer?	☐	☐	35
Are any audit committee members company employees?	☐	☐	36
Is any portion of your company not open to internal audit?	☐	☐	37
If answer is "yes", please describe.			38-39
_____			
_____			
_____			40-41
In your opinion has internal control in your firm received more emphasis since audit committees were mandated?	☐	☐	42

The next two questions refer to computerzied operations.

Question No. 13

With regard to your firm's computerized operations, please do the following two things. First, please indicate with a "1" the organizational level which has primary responsibility for the following. Second, check the boxes indicating the other organizational level(s) which are also involved.

	Chief Financial Officer/ Controller	Line Manager	Internal Audit Manager	Data Processing Manager	
Assigning organizational responsibility for computerized systems	☐	☐	☐	☐	43-46
Responsibility for acquisition of computerized systems	☐	☐	☐	☐	47-50
Cost control over development and operations	☐	☐	☐	☐	51-54
Measuring efficiency and effectiveness of computerized systems	☐	☐	☐	☐	55-58
Assuring reliable computer security	☐	☐	☐	☐	59-62
Audit of data processing activities	☐	☐	☐	☐	63-66
Design of computerized systems	☐	☐	☐	☐	67-70
Responsibility for integrity of operating data	☐	☐	☐	☐	6-9
Assuring that adequate internal controls are built into computerized systems	☐	☐	☐	☐	10-13
Authorizing changes to computerized systems.	☐	☐	☐	☐	14-17

Question No. 14

	Yes	No	
Is there provision for general staff training in data processing for managers in the company not familiar with information systems?	☐	☐	18
Does your firm provide for a search for new computer applications which will protect the company's competitive advantage?	☐	☐	19
Is there a budget for this kind of activity?	☐	☐	20
Are there specific goals and objectives established for computerized information systems?	☐	☐	21
Is there a charge-back system for data processing costs?	☐	☐	22
If yes, is this a full-cost charge-back?	☐	☐	23
Have advancement opportunities within the company for the Chief Information Officer (Data Processing Manager) been provided for?	☐	☐	24

PART II

These questions involve your assessment of your company's internal control practices. This section is designed to assess internal control generally. No specific corporations will be identified.

Question No. 15

Check the box that best describes your:	Internal Control System	Internal Audit System	Internal Audit of Computerized System	
Excellent – includes all measures that can be justified on a cost-effective basis.	☐	☐	☐	25-27
Approaching excellence – final improvements are either in process of implementation or under consideration.	☐	☐	☐	
Satisfactory – needs minor improvement.	☐	☐	☐	
Needs major improvement.	☐	☐	☐	
Other (please explain)	☐	☐	☐	

Question No. 16

	Yes	No	
Is provision made within your company for monitoring of compliance with internal control procedures?	☐	☐	28
If "yes", is compliance monitoring			
Excessive?	☐	☐	29
About right?	☐	☐	30
Less than desirable?	☐	☐	31
Is compliance monitoring provided by:			
Internal audit function?	☐	☐	32
Controller's department?	☐	☐	33
Systems specialists?	☐	☐	34
Independent external auditors?	☐	☐	35
Other (please explain	☐	☐	36
_____			37-38
_____			39-40
_____			

Question No. 17

	Yes	No	
Is the quality of internal control consistent throughout your company?	☐	☐	41

If the answer is "No", rank up to five reasons which might account for this inconsistency (1=most important). Please do not assign tied ranks.

Lack of management attention.	☐	42-51
Characteristics of the parent company.	☐	
Changes in key personnel.	☐	
General personnel turnover.	☐	
Differing standards of appropriate conduct arising from dissimilar cultural backgrounds.	☐	
Geographic disperson.	☐	
Recent business acquisitions.	☐	
Characteristics of a specific division or unit, for example, maturity, nature of activity or business, organizational structures.	☐	
Characteristics of the division or unit staff, for example, size, quality of personnel, extent of training.	☐	
Other (please explain)	☐	52-53
_____		
_____		
_____		

Question No. 18

Select from the following, the five strongest features of your internal control system and rank them in order (1=strongest). Please do not assign tied ranks.

Control measures specifically designed for our most sensitive or otherwise important control problems. ☐	54-63
Company traditions and customs. ☐	
Quality of our personnel. ☐	
Attitude of top management. ☐	
Special attention to electronic data processing controls. ☐	
Monitoring of compliance with internal control measures. ☐	
A widespread awareness that control measures exist. ☐	
Formal control procedures such as separation of duties, independent reviews, reconciliations, and evaluations. ☐	
An active internal audit department. ☐	
Other (please explain) ☐	
_____	64-65
_____	
_____	

Question No. 19

What do you consider to be the type of transaction or activity within your company for which adequate internal control is most important? (Check up to three most important.)

Purchasing ☐	66-71
Sales ☐	
Cash disbursements ☐	
International operations ☐	
Cash receipts ☐	
Inventory and materials handling ☐	
Payroll ☐	
Commission, royalty, or other variable payments ☐	
Processing of computerized data ☐	
Other (describe briefly) ☐	
_____	72-73
_____	
Other (describe briefly) ☐	
_____	74-75
_____	

Question No. 20

This question is designed to assess perceptions of risk.

From an *internal control* point of view, which of your company's activities now cause you the greatest concern?

	Of Major Concern	Of Some Concern	Not A Concern	
Decentralized operations	☐	☐	☐	6
Electronic data processing	☐	☐	☐	7
Production quality control	☐	☐	☐	8
Foreign operations	☐	☐	☐	9
Purchasing	☐	☐	☐	10
Marketing	☐	☐	☐	11
Budgeting	☐	☐	☐	12
Research and development	☐	☐	☐	13
Compliance with government regulations	☐	☐	☐	14
Financing activities	☐	☐	☐	15
External financial reporting	☐	☐	☐	16
Inventory, receiving, shipping and materials handling	☐	☐	☐	17
Construction and contracting	☐	☐	☐	18
Product pricing	☐	☐	☐	19
Payroll	☐	☐	☐	20
Investment	☐	☐	☐	21
New or greatly expanding company operations	☐	☐	☐	22
Other (describe briefly)	☐	☐	☐	23
_____				24-25
_____				

Question No. 21

	Yes	No	
Do specific characteristics of your company make internal control unusually difficult to maintain at an adequate level?	☐	☐	26

If you answered "yes", please check any of the following which account for this:

Too much rotation of personnel.	☐	27
Rapid growth of your company or industry.	☐	28
Constant changes in products or services.	☐	29
Frequent acquisitions.	☐	30
Geographic dispersion.	☐	31
Decentralization.	☐	32
Need for local management autonomy.	☐	33
Resistance by highly technical or creative personnel.	☐	34
Diversity of business segments.	☐	35
Competitive management.	☐	36
Attitude of top management.	☐	37
Small size of staff.	☐	38
Governmental regulations.	☐	39
Foreign operations.	☐	40
Labour relations.	☐	41
Other	☐	42
_____		43-44
_____		45-46

Question No. 22

This question is designed to identify management's perceptions of potential risks associated with computerized operations within their firms. Of the following issues, please indicate your perceptions of their potential risk within your company.

	A Significant Potential Problem	A Minor Problem	Not a Problem	
Maintaining an adequate audit trail.	☐	☐	☐	47
Ability to audit the actual programs.	☐	☐	☐	48
Not sufficiently involving internal audit with the establishment of data processing systems.	☐	☐	☐	49
Ability of internal audit to audit data processing operations.	☐	☐	☐	50
Ability of external audit to audit data processing operations.	☐	☐	☐	51
Locating data processing personnel with sufficient expertise.	☐	☐	☐	52
Not sufficiently involving operating management with the establishment of data processing systems.	☐	☐	☐	53
Cost control of data processing operations.	☐	☐	☐	54
Monitoring effectiveness and efficiency of computerized systems.	☐	☐	☐	55
Transmission of computerized data over telephone or satellite.	☐	☐	☐	56
Having a recovery plan in case of hardware destruction.	☐	☐	☐	57
Testing of such a recovery program.	☐	☐	☐	58

Question No. 23

	Yes	No	
Are you generally satisfied with the service provided by your external auditor for:			
Audit of financial information?	☐	☐	59
Audit of computerized operations?	☐	☐	60
(Please explain) _____			
_____			
_____			

Question No. 24

If there are any special strengths or weaknesses of your company's internal control system that you feel should be included in its evaluation, please describe them briefly here. Add supplementary sheets if necessary.

_____

_____

_____

As part of this research project, we plan to make a study of the content and emphasis in corporate codes of officer and employee conduct. If you have such a code, could you please include two copies when you return your questionnaire. Any codes you send us will be treated as confidentially as your answers to the questionnaire.

Thank you for your participation. It is very much appreciated.

RESEARCH PROJECT ON INTERNAL CONTROL IN CANADIAN CORPORATIONS

sponsored jointly by

CANADIAN INSTITUTE OF CHARTERED ACCOUNTANTS	AND	SOCIETY OF MANAGEMENT ACCOUNTANTS OF CANADA

INTERNAL AUDIT MANAGER QUESTIONNAIRE

INTRODUCTION

The topic of "Internal Control in Canadian Corporations" has been selected by the Canadian Institute of Chartered Accountants and the Society of Management Accountants as a topic of sufficient importance for their first jointly sponsored research study. Its emphasis is upon internal control from management's perspective.

The objectives of the study are to: explore management's understanding of internal control, to examine how it is practiced in top Canadian corporations, to identify risk factors, and to determine who is responsible for various aspects. This will also be the first Canadian study to conduct an empirical examination of the role played by computerized information systems in internal control of the large corporation, and to assess risks created by this new technology. It is anticipated that the findings of this study should substantially assist Canadian companies in assessing their own internal control practices.

This research is not intended to discover some idealized version of internal control or to evaluate your company's control system. Its purpose is to determine actual practice. You will make a significant contribution to its success if you just "tell it like it is".

With very few exceptions, the questions can be answered by placing a check mark or a rating number in one of the boxes provided. Please read the question completely before beginning to answer.

Please return within ten days to: Dr. L.D. Etherington
Dr. I.M. Gordon
Faculty of Business Administration
Simon Fraser University
Burnaby, B.C.
V5A 1S6

Demographic Data:

Sex ☐ Male ☐ Female   7

	Yes	No	
Academic Degree	☐	☐	8
If yes, please specify _____			9-14
Professional Designation	☐	☐	15
If yes, please specify _____			16-21

Number of years with this firm _____   22-23
Number of years in internal audit _____   24-25

Age ☐ Under 35 ☐ 35-45 ☐ 46-55 ☐ 56 or Over   28

Industry Information:

Industry: Retailing ☐   Transportation ☐
Manufacturing ☐   Forestry ☐   29
Mining ☐   Utilities ☐
Petrol. & Energy ☐   Financial Services ☐
Other ☐

(Please specify) _____   30-31

Size of firm within your industry: ☐ Large ☐ Medium ☐ Small   32

Are you within a regulated industry?   Yes ☐   No ☐   33

PART I

These questions are intended to discover the extent of the internal control practices now employed within your company.

Question No. 1

To what extent does your company acknowledge the existence of a control system by referring to it in policy letters, management statements, delegation of authority and job descriptions?

☐ Extensively   ☐ To some extent   ☐ Not at all   34

Question No. 2

Check the boxes indicating the organizational level(s) at which the following occur:

	Designs Internal Control System	Approves the System	Evaluates Systems Effectiveness	Authorizes Changes to the System	
Controller or Chief Accounting Officer	☐	☐	☐	☐	35-38
Chief Financial Officer	☐	☐	☐	☐	39-42
Internal Audit Manager	☐	☐	☐	☐	43-46
Chief Executive Officer	☐	☐	☐	☐	47-50
External Auditor	☐	☐	☐	☐	51-54
Audit Committee or Board	☐	☐	☐	☐	55-58

Question No. 3

Is a comprehensive effort made to inform officers and employees of:

	Officer and Key employees		Other employees		
	Yes	No	Yes	No	
Company objectives?	☐	☐	☐	☐	59-60
Their personal responsibilities?	☐	☐	☐	☐	61-62
Applicable internal control measures?	☐	☐	☐	☐	63-64

Question No. 4

Please indicate your perception of the importance of the following objectives of a system of internal control:

	Very Important	Somewhat Important	Of Little Importance	Not Important	
Prevention and detection of fraud.	☐	☐	☐	☐	65
Prevention and detection of error.	☐	☐	☐	☐	66
Ensuring orderly and efficient conduct of business.	☐	☐	☐	☐	67
Discharging statutory responsibilities to owners.	☐	☐	☐	☐	68
Safeguarding of assets.	☐	☐	☐	☐	69
Profitability and minimization of costs.	☐	☐	☐	☐	70
Assuring effective use of company resources.	☐	☐	☐	☐	71
Ensuring reliability of accounting records.	☐	☐	☐	☐	72
Timely preparation of financial statements.	☐	☐	☐	☐	73
Ensuring compliance with management policies.	☐	☐	☐	☐	74
Other (please specify)	☐	☐	☐	☐	75

Question No. 5

How large is your internal audit staff, including yourself? _____ 6-7

	Yes	No	
Does the chief internal auditor have organizational independence (i.e., not dependent for job, pay, or promotion purposes) from those responsible for the activities audited?	☐	☐	8
Do you have an audit comittee?	☐	☐	9
Does the internal audit function have access to the Board of Directors or the Corporate Audit Committee without requiring approval from any company officer?	☐	☐	10
Are any audit committee members company employees?	☐	☐	11
Is any portion of your company not open to internal audit?	☐	☐	12

If answer is "yes", please describe.

_____ 13-14

_____ 15-16

In your opinion has internal control in your firm received more emphasis since audit committees were mandated? ☐ ☐ 17

Question No. 6

	Yes	No	
Is the internal audit department seen as an entry-level department for new financial management recruits?	☐	☐	18

If yes, then what is the average number of years spent in internal audit by new recruits? _____ 19-20

What educational and/or professional credentials do new recruits usually possess? (Please check all that apply.)

Bachelor's degree in Business	☐	21
Bachelor's degree in Computing Science	☐	22
Other bachelor's degree	☐	23
(Please specify) _____		24-27
CA	☐	28
CGA	☐	29
RIA	☐	30
Other professional designation	☐	31
(Please specify) _____		32-35

Question No. 7

	Yes	No	
Is there any internal audit team member(s) who is designated as a computerized information system audit specialist?	☐	☐	36

If yes, what is the average number of years spent in internal audit by such a person? _____ 37-38

Was this person hired internally? ☐ ☐ 39

If yes, what department previously employed this person? (please specify) _____ 40-41

Please indicate the educational and/or professional credentials such a specialist may usually have?

Bachelor's degree in Business	☐	42
Bachelor's degree in Computing Science	☐	43
Other bachelor's degree	☐	44
(Please specify) _____		45-48
CA	☐	49
CGA	☐	50
RIA	☐	51
Other	☐	52
(Please specify) _____		53-56

Question No. 8

Who approves your annual audit program?	Yes	No	
CFO	☐	☐	57
Audit Committee	☐	☐	58
External Auditor	☐	☐	59
Other (please specify)	☐	☐	60
_____			61-62

Question No. 9

What is the auditee's role in internal audit?	Yes	No	
Auditee consulted prior to beginning audit re specific requests.	☐	☐	63
Auditee consulted prior to completion of audit report.	☐	☐	64
Auditee has option of not concurring with findings of recommendations.	☐	☐	65
Auditee has mandatory follow-up requirement.	☐	☐	66

Question No. 10

Who receives your audit reports?			
CFO	☐	☐	67
Audit Committee	☐	☐	68
External auditor	☐	☐	69
Auditee	☐	☐	70
Auditee's Vice-President	☐	☐	71
Other (please specify)	☐	☐	72
_____			73-74
_____			75-76

Question No. 11

How is internal audit evaluated?	Yes	No	
Feedback from auditees	☐	☐	6
Company savings achieved	☐	☐	7
Judgment of CFO	☐	☐	8
Audits by parent	☐	☐	9
Other (please specify)	☐	☐	10
_____			11-12

Are you generally satisfied with how you are evaluated? ☐ ☐ 13

(Please explain if required.)

_____ 14-15

Question No. 12

How much of internal audit's resources are devoted to auditing the following?

	Percent	
Financial statement information	☐	16-17
Operational audit	☐	18-19
Computerized systems	☐	20-21
Special audits	☐	22-23
Other	☐	24-25

	Yes	No	
Does external audit rely on internal audit department's work to any significant degree?	☐	☐	26
If yes, has this decreased external audit fees in the past two years?	☐	☐	27
By what percentage? _____%			28-29

Question No. 13

To what extent is your internal control system described in company manuals?

Completely	☐	30
Almost completely	☐	
Partially	☐	
Very little	☐	
Other (please explain)	☐	
_____		31-32

	Yes	No	
Are responsibilities of different positions and levels of authority clearly stated in company manuals or instructions?	☐	☐	33

Question No. 14

Check the boxes indicating the organizational level(s) at which the following occur:

	Reports on Internal Control to Financial Management	Reports on Internal Control to Senior Management	Reports on Internal Control to Board or Audit Committee	Receives Data Processing Manager's Report	
Chief Executive Officer	☐	☐	☐	☐	34-37
Chief Financial Officer	☐	☐	☐	☐	38-41
Controller	☐	☐	☐	☐	42-45
Internal Audit	☐	☐	☐	☐	46-49
External Audit	☐	☐	☐	☐	50-53
Line Manager	☐	☐	☐	☐	54-57

Question No. 15

Indicate (a) the extent to which each type of expenditure listed below is or is not restricted as to amount in the normal course of business, and (b) the level of approval required (such as independent senior officer, Committee of Directors, or full Board) to exceed the imposed limit, if any.

	(a) Nature of Limit			(b) Level of Approval Required to Exceed Limit	
	None	Budgeted Amount	Fixed Maximum Amount		
Operating expenditures	☐	☐	☐	_____	58,59-60
Inventory purchases	☐	☐	☐	_____	61,62-63
Capital expenditures	☐	☐	☐	_____	64,65-66
Incurrence of debt: Under one year	☐	☐	☐	_____	67,68-69
More than one year	☐	☐	☐	_____	70,71-72
Contracts to sell or provide service	☐	☐	☐	_____	73,74-75

Question No. 16

	Formal Analysis	Informal Analysis	No Analysis	
Does your company make a cost benefit analysis before introducing significant changes in internal control?	☐	☐	☐	76

Question No. 17

With regard to your firm's computerized operations, please do the following two things. First, please indicate with a "1" the organizational level which has primary responsibility for the following. Second, check the boxes indicating the other organizational level(s) which are also involved.

	Chief Financial Officer/ Controller	Line Manager	Internal Audit Manager	Data Processing Manager	
Assigning organizational responsibility for computerized systems	☐	☐	☐	☐	6-9
Cost control over development and operations	☐	☐	☐	☐	10-13
Measuring efficiency and effectiveness of computerized systems	☐	☐	☐	☐	14-17
Assuring reliable computer security	☐	☐	☐	☐	18-21
Audit of data processing activities	☐	☐	☐	☐	22-25
Design of computerized systems	☐	☐	☐	☐	26-29
Sign-offs of computerized systems	☐	☐	☐	☐	30-33
Responsibility for integrity of operating data	☐	☐	☐	☐	34-37
Assuring that adequate internal controls are built into computerized systems	☐	☐	☐	☐	38-41
Authorizing changes to computerized systems.	☐	☐	☐	☐	42-45

Question No. 18

	Yes	No	
Does your firm classify computerized data according to its sensitivity and institute controls accordingly?	☐	☐	46

PART II

These questions involve your assessment of your company's internal control practices. This section is designed to assess internal control in Canadian Corporations generally.

Question No. 19

Check the box that best describes your:	Internal Control System	Internal Audit System	Internal Audit of Computerized System	
Excellent – includes all measures that can be justified on a cost-effective basis.	☐	☐	☐	47-49
Approaching excellence – final improvements are either in process of implementation or under consideration.	☐	☐	☐	
Satisfactory – needs minor improvement.	☐	☐	☐	
Needs major improvement.	☐	☐	☐	
Other (please explain)	☐	☐	☐	

_____

_____

Question No. 20

	Yes	No	
Is provision made within your company for monitoring of compliance with internal control procedures?	☐	☐	50
If "yes", is compliance monitoring			
Excessive?	☐	☐	51
About right?	☐	☐	52
Less than desirable?	☐	☐	53
Is compliance monitoring provided by:			
Internal audit function?	☐	☐	54
Controller's department?	☐	☐	55
Systems specialists?	☐	☐	56
Independent external auditors?	☐	☐	57
Other (please explain	☐	☐	58

_____ 59-60

_____ 61-62

_____ 63-64

Question No. 21

Select from the following the five strongest features of your internal control system and rank them in order (1=strongest). Please do not assign tied ranks.

Control measures specifically designed for our most sensitive or otherwise important control problems.	☐	65-74
Company traditions and customs.	☐	
Quality of our personnel.	☐	
Attitude of top management.	☐	
Special attention to electronic data processing controls.	☐	
Monitoring of compliance with internal control measures.	☐	
A widespread awareness that control measures exist.	☐	
Formal control procedures such as separation of duties, independent reviews, reconciliations, and evaluations.	☐	
An active internal audit department.	☐	
Other (please explain)	☐	

_____ 75-76

_____

_____

Question No. 22

What do you consider to be the type of transaction or activity within your company for which adequate internal control is most important? (Check up to three most important.)

Purchasing	☐	6-11
Sales	☐	
Cash disbursements	☐	
International operations	☐	
Cash receipts	☐	
Inventory and materials handling	☐	
Payroll	☐	
Commission, royalty or other variable payments	☐	
Processing of computerized data	☐	
Other (describe briefly)	☐	

_____   12-13

Other (describe briefly)   ☐

_____   14-15

Question No. 23

This question is designed to assess perceptions of risk.

From an internal control point of view, which of your company's activities now cause you the greatest concern?

	Of Major Concern	Of Some Concern	Not A Concern	
Decentralized operations	☐	☐	☐	16
Electronic data processing	☐	☐	☐	17
Production quality control	☐	☐	☐	18
Foreign operations	☐	☐	☐	19
Purchasing	☐	☐	☐	20
Marketing	☐	☐	☐	21
Budgeting	☐	☐	☐	22
Research and development	☐	☐	☐	23
Compliance with government regulations	☐	☐	☐	24
Financing activities	☐	☐	☐	25
External financial reporting	☐	☐	☐	26
Inventory, receiving, shipping and materials handling	☐	☐	☐	27
Construction and contracting	☐	☐	☐	28
Product pricing	☐	☐	☐	29
Payroll	☐	☐	☐	30
Investment	☐	☐	☐	31
New or greatly expanding company operations	☐	☐	☐	32
Other (describe briefly)	☐	☐	☐	33

_____   34-35

_____   36-37

Question No. 24

	Yes	No	
Is the quality of internal control consistent throughout your company?	☐	☐	38
Do specific characteristics of your company make internal control unusually difficult to maintain at an adequate level?	☐	☐	39

If you answered "yes" to the second question, please check any of the following which account for this:

Too much rotation of personnel.	☐	40
Rapid growth of your company or industry.	☐	41
Constant changes in products or services.	☐	42
Frequest acquisitions.	☐	43
Geographic dispersion.	☐	44
Decentralization.	☐	45
Need for local management autonomy.	☐	46
Resistance by highly technical or creative personnel.	☐	47
Diversity of business segments.	☐	48
Competitive management.	☐	49
Attitude of top management.	☐	50
Small size of staff.	☐	51
Governmental regulations.	☐	52
Foreign operations.	☐	53
Labour relations.	☐	54
Other	☐	55

_____   56-57

_____   58-59

Question No. 25

	Yes	No	
Is internal auditing perceived by others as a:			
Policeman?	☐	☐	60
Consultant?	☐	☐	61
Are you generally satisfied with this perception?	☐	☐	62

(Please explain) _____   63-64

_____

_____

Question No. 26

	Yes	No	
Are you generally satisfied with the service provided by your external auditor for:			
Audit of financial information?	☐	☐	65
Audit of computerized operations?	☐	☐	66

(Please explain) _____

_____   67-68

_____

Question No. 27

This question is designed to identify management's perceptions of potential risks associated with computerized operations within their firms. Of the following issues, please indicate your perceptions of their potential risk within your company.

	A Significant Potential Problem	A Minor Problem	Not a Problem	
Maintaining an adequate audit trail.	☐	☐	☐	69
Ability to audit the actual programs.	☐	☐	☐	70
Not sufficiently involving internal audit with the establishment of data processing systems.	☐	☐	☐	71
Ability of internal audit to audit data processing operations.	☐	☐	☐	72
Ability of external audit to audit data processing operations.	☐	☐	☐	73
Locating internal audit personnel with sufficient expertise.	☐	☐	☐	74
Restricting access to computer information	☐	☐	☐	75
Cost control of data processing operations.	☐	☐	☐	76
Monitoring effectiveness and efficiency of computerized systems.	☐	☐	☐	77
Transmission of computerized data over telephone or satellite.	☐	☐	☐	78
Ensuring access and security of computer facilities and backup files.	☐	☐	☐	6
Keeping backup files current.	☐	☐	☐	7
Having a recovery plan in case of hardware destruction.	☐	☐	☐	8
Testing of such a recovery program.	☐	☐	☐	9

Question No. 28

If there are any special strengths or weaknesses of your company's internal control system that you feel should be included in its evaluation, please describe them briefly here. Add supplementary sheets if necessary.

_____

_____

_____

_____

Thank you for your participation. It is very much appreciated.

RESEARCH PROJECT ON INTERNAL CONTROL IN CANADIAN CORPORATIONS

sponsored jointly by

CANADIAN INSTITUTE OF CHARTERED ACCOUNTANTS	AND	SOCIETY OF MANAGEMENT ACCOUNTANTS OF CANADA

DATA PROCESSING MANAGER QUESTIONNAIRE

INTRODUCTION

The topic of "Internal Control in Canadian Corporations" has been selected by the Canadian Institute of Chartered Accountants and the Society of Management Accountants as a topic of sufficient importance for their first jointly sponsored research study. Its emphasis is upon internal control from management's perspective.

The objectives of the study are to: explore management's understanding of internal control, to examine how it is practiced in top Canadian corporations, to identify risk factors, and to determine who is responsible for various aspects. This will also be the first Canadian study to conduct an empirical examination of the role played by computerized information systems in internal control of the large corporation, and to assess risks created by this new technology. It is anticipated that the findings of this study should substantially assist Canadian companies in assessing their own internal control practices.

This research is not intended to discover some idealized version of internal control or to evaluate your company's internal control system. Its purpose is to determine actual practice. You will make a significant contribution to its success if you just "tell it like it is".

With very few exceptions, the questions can be answered by placing a check mark or a rating number in one of the boxes provided. Please read the question completely before beginning to answer.

Please return within ten days to: Dr. L.D. Etherington
Dr. I.M. Gordon
Faculty of Business Administration
Simon Fraser University
Burnaby, B.C.
V5A 1S6

Demographic Data:

Sex ☐ ☐
Male Female   7

	Yes	No	
Academic Degree	☐	☐	8
If yes, please specify _____			9-14
Professional Designation	☐	☐	15
If yes, please specify _____			16-21

Number of years with this firm _____   22-23

Number of years in data processing _____   24-25

Number of years with this firm as
data processing manager _____   26-27

Age ☐ ☐ ☐ ☐   28
Under 35   35-45   46-55   56 or Over

Industry Information:

Industry: Retailing ☐   Transportation ☐
Manufacturing ☐   Forestry ☐   29
Mining ☐   Utilities ☐
Petrol. & Energy ☐ Financial Services ☐
Other ☐
(Please specify) _____   30-31

Size of firm within ☐ ☐ ☐   32
your industry: Large   Medium   Small

Are you within a   Yes   No
regulated industry?   ☐ ☐   33

PART I

These questions are intended to discover the extent of the internal control practices now employed within your company.

Question No. 1

To what extent does your company acknowledge the existence of a control system by referring to it in policy letters, management statements, delegation of authority and job descriptions?

☐ ☐ ☐   34
Extensively   To some extent   Not at all

Question No. 2

Is a comprehensive effort made to inform officers and employees of:

	Officer and Key employees		Other employees		
	Yes	No	Yes	No	
Company objectives?	☐	☐	☐	☐	35-36
Their personal responsibilities?	☐	☐	☐	☐	37-38
Applicable internal control measures?	☐	☐	☐	☐	39-40

Question No. 3

What educational and/or professional credentials do new data processing recruits usually possess? (Please check all that apply.)

Bachelor's degree in Business	☐	41
Bachelor's degree in Computing Science	☐	42
Other bachelor's degree	☐	43
(Please specify) _____		44
Professional designation	☐	45
(Please specify) _____		46
Other	☐	47-48
(Please specify) _____		49-50

Question No. 4

	Yes	No	
Is there provision for general staff training in data processing for managers in the company not familiar with information systems?	☐	☐	51
Does your firm provide for a search for new computer applications which will protect the company's competitive advantage?	☐	☐	52
Is there a budget for this kind of activity?	☐	☐	53
Are there specific goals and objectives established for computerized information systems?	☐	☐	54
Is there a charge-back system for data processing costs?	☐	☐	55
If yes, is this a full-cost charge-back?	☐	☐	56
Do you purchase any computer services from outside your firm?	☐	☐	57
Does your firm classify computerized data according to its sensitivity and institute controls accordingly?	☐	☐	58
Are there trade journals which discuss special adaptations of the computer to your industry problems?	☐	☐	59
Are microcomputers used within your company for stand-alone functions?	☐	☐	60

Question No. 5

	Yes	No	
Is there any internal audit team member who is designated as a computerized information system audit specialist?	☐	☐	61
Are data processing specialists rotated into internal audit to act as technical consultants?	☐	☐	62
If yes, what is the average number of years spent in internal audit by this person? _____			63-64
Are some of your staff hired internally?	☐	☐	65
If yes, what department(s) would previously have employed these staff persons? (Please specify) _____			66-67
Does your firm have a coordinating committee for computerized systems?	☐	☐	68

Question No. 6

	Yes	No	
Does a specific job description exist for your position?	☐	☐	69
Are responsibilities of different positions and levels of authority clearly stated in company manuals or instructions?	☐	☐	70
Have advancement opportunities within the company for the Chief Information Officer (Data Processing Manager) been provided for?	☐	☐	71

Question No. 7

	Yes	No	
Do operating departments participate in the budget planning process for computerized information systems?	☐	☐	72
Are actual results of your department compared with budgeted results?	☐	☐	73
Is explanation of any material differences documented?	☐	☐	74
At what levels are such explanations reviewed?			
Board of Directors	☐	☐	75
Corporate management	☐	☐	76
Divisional management	☐	☐	77
Unit or department management	☐	☐	78

Question No. 8

To what extent is your department's internal control system described in company manuals? (Please check the appropriate box.)

Completely	☐	
Almost completely	☐	6
Partially	☐	
Very little	☐	
Other (please explain)	☐	

_____

_____ 7

Question No. 9

With regard to your firm's computerized operations, please do the following two things. First, please indicate with a "1" the organizational level which has primary responsibility for the following. Second, check the boxes indicating the other organizational level(s) which are also involved.

	Chief Financial Officer/ Controller	Line Manager	Internal Audit Manager	Data Processing Manager	
Assigning organizational responsibility for computerized systems	☐	☐	☐	☐	8-11
Responsibility for acquisition of computerized systems	☐	☐	☐	☐	12-15
Assimilating computerized systems into the company	☐	☐	☐	☐	16-19
Cost control over development and operations	☐	☐	☐	☐	20-23
Measuring efficiency and effectiveness of computerized systems	☐	☐	☐	☐	24-27
Assuring reliable computer security	☐	☐	☐	☐	28-31
Audit of data processing activities	☐	☐	☐	☐	32-35
Design of computerized systems	☐	☐	☐	☐	36-39
Sign-offs of computerized systems	☐	☐	☐	☐	40-43
Responsibility for integrity of operating data	☐	☐	☐	☐	44-47
Assuring that adequate internal controls are built into computerized systems	☐	☐	☐	☐	48-51
Authorizing changes to computerized systems.	☐	☐	☐	☐	52-55

Question No. 10

To whom do you report?

	Yes	No	
Chief Executive Officer	☐	☐	56
Chief Financial Officer	☐	☐	57
Controller	☐	☐	58
Other (please specify)	☐	☐	59
_____			60-61
_____			

To whom do you report on internal control?

	Yes	No	
Senior management	☐	☐	62
Internal audit	☐	☐	63
External audit	☐	☐	64
Other (please specify)	☐	☐	65
_____			66-67
_____			

Question No. 11

Using approximate percentages, indicate the major users of computerized systems in your company for the past (1975-1981), present (1982-1983), and the future (1984-1989).

	Past	Present	Future	
Finance	☐ %	☐ %	☐ %	6-11
Accounting	☐	☐	☐	12-17
Engineering	☐	☐	☐	18-23
Inventory	☐	☐	☐	24-29
Manufacturing	☐	☐	☐	30-35
Distribution	☐	☐	☐	36-41
General Support (or Corporate)	☐	☐	☐	42-47
Personnel	☐	☐	☐	48-53
Marketing	☐	☐	☐	54-59
Other (please specify)	☐	☐	☐	60-65
_____				
_____				66-71
	100%	100%	100%	

Question No. 12

How is the data processing department evaluated?

	Yes	No	
Feedback from operating departments	☐	☐	6
Feedback from financial management	☐	☐	7
Feedback from internal audit	☐	☐	8
Evaluation of external auditors	☐	☐	9
Judgment of your superior	☐	☐	10
Judgment of CEO	☐	☐	11
Keeping within budget	☐	☐	12
Development of new applications	☐	☐	13
Other (please specify)	☐	☐	14
			15-16

_____

_____

	Yes	No	
Other (please specify)	☐	☐	17
			18-19

_____

_____

	Yes	No	
Are you generally satisfied with how data processing is evaluated?	☐	☐	20

(Please explain if required.)

_____ 21

_____

_____

_____

Question No. 13

What is the extent of your company's reliance on the computer for the following?

	Totally Reliant	Significantly Reliant	Somewhat Reliant	Not Significantly Reliant	
Financial and accounting data	☐	☐	☐	☐	22
Personnel	☐	☐	☐	☐	23
Operations	☐	☐	☐	☐	24
Manufacturing	☐	☐	☐	☐	25
Inventory	☐	☐	☐	☐	26
Engineering	☐	☐	☐	☐	27
Research & Development	☐	☐	☐	☐	28
Planning	☐	☐	☐	☐	29
Other business information	☐	☐	☐	☐	30

Question No. 14

	Formal Analysis	Informal Analysis	No Analysis	
Does your company make a formal cost benefit analysis before introducing significant changes in internal control?	☐	☐	☐	31

PART II

These questions involve your assessment of your company's internal control practices. This section is designed to assess internal control in Canadian corporations generally. No specific corporation will be identified.

Question No. 15

Check the box that best describes your:	Internal Control System	External Audit of Computerized Systems	Internal Audit of Computerized Systems	
Excellent – includes all measures that can be justified on a cost-effective basis.	☐	☐	☐	32-34
Approaching excellence – final improvements are either in process of implementation or under consideration.	☐	☐	☐	
Satisfactory – needs minor improvement.	☐	☐	☐	
Needs major improvement.	☐	☐	☐	
Other (please explain)	☐	☐	☐	

_____

_____

Question No. 16

	Yes	No	
Is provision made within your company for monitoring of compliance with internal control procedures?	☐	☐	35

If "yes", is compliance monitoring

	Yes	No	
Excessive?	☐	☐	36
About right?	☐	☐	37
Less than desirable?	☐	☐	38

Is compliance monitoring provided by:

	Yes	No	
Internal audit function?	☐	☐	39
Controller's department?	☐	☐	40
Systems specialists?	☐	☐	41
Independent external auditors?	☐	☐	42
Other (please explain)	☐	☐	43
			44-45

_____ 46-47

_____ 48-49

_____

Question No. 17

Select from the following, the five strongest features of your department's internal control system and rank them in order (1=strongest). Please do not assign tied ranks.

Control measures specifically designed for our most sensitive or otherwise important control problems.	☐	50-59
Company traditions and customs.	☐	
Quality of our personnel.	☐	
Attitude of top management.	☐	
Monitoring of compliance with internal control measures.	☐	
A widespread awareness that control measures exist.	☐	
Formal control procedures such as separation of duties, independent reviews, reconciliations, and evaluations.	☐	
An active internal audit department.	☐	
Other (please explain)	☐	
		60-61

_____

_____

Question No. 18

This question is designed to identify management's perceptions of potential risks associated with computerized operations within their firms. Of the following issues, please indicate your perceptions of their potential risk within your company.

	A Significant Potential Problem	A Minor Problem	Not a Problem	
Maintaining an adequate audit trail.	☐	☐	☐	62
Ability to audit the actual programs.	☐	☐	☐	63
Not sufficiently involving internal audit with the establishment of data processing systems.	☐	☐	☐	64
Ability of internal audit to audit data processing operations.	☐	☐	☐	65
Locating data processing personnel with sufficient expertise.	☐	☐	☐	66
Distributing data processing.	☐	☐	☐	67
Not sufficiently involving operating management with the establishment of data processing systems.	☐	☐	☐	68
Restricting access to computer information.	☐	☐	☐	69
Cost control of data processing operations.	☐	☐	☐	70
Monitoring effectiveness and efficiency of computerized systems.	☐	☐	☐	71
Transmission of computerized data over telephone or satellite.	☐	☐	☐	72
Ensuring access and security of computer facilities and backup files.	☐	☐	☐	73
Keeping backup files current.	☐	☐	☐	74
Having a recovery plan in case of hardware destruction.	☐	☐	☐	75
Testing of such a recovery program.	☐	☐	☐	76

Question No. 19

	Yes	No	
Is the quality of internal control of computerized systems consistent throughout your company?	☐	☐	77
Do specific characteristics of your company make internal control of data processing unusually difficult to maintain at an adequate level?	☐	☐	78

If you answered "yes" to the second question, please check any of the following which account for this:

Too much rotation of personnel.	☐	6
Rapid growth of your company or industry.	☐	7
Constant changes in products or services.	☐	8
Frequent acquisitions.	☐	9
Geographic dispersion.	☐	10
Decentralization.	☐	11
Need for local management autonomy.	☐	12
Resistance by highly technical or creative personnel.	☐	13
Diversity of business segments.	☐	14
Competitive management.	☐	15
Attitude of top management.	☐	16
Small size of staff.	☐	17
Governmental regulations.	☐	18
Foreign operations.	☐	19
Labour relations.	☐	20
Other	☐	21
		22-23
		24-25

Question No. 20

Does your department view internal auditing as a:

	Yes	No	
Policeman?	☐	☐	26
Consultant?	☐	☐	27
Spy for top management?	☐	☐	28
Other (please specify)	☐	☐	29
			30-31
			32-33

Question No. 21

	Yes	No	
Are you generally satisfied with the service provided by your external auditor for audit of computerized information systems:	☐	☐	34
If not, please explain.			35-36

Question No. 22

Would you rate your current data processing hardware as:

	Yes	No	
Capable of meeting anticipated needs over the next 5 years?	☐	☐	37
Sufficient to meet present needs?	☐	☐	38
Becoming obsolete?	☐	☐	39
Obsolete?	☐	☐	40

Would you rate your current data processing software as:

	Yes	No	
Capable of meeting anticipated needs over the next 5 years?	☐	☐	41
Sufficient to meet present needs?	☐	☐	42
Becoming obsolete?	☐	☐	43
Obsolete?	☐	☐	44

Question No. 23

Computerization of your firm compared with others in your industry is:

☐	☐	☐	☐	☐	45
Substantially Greater	Somewhat Greater	About the Same	Somewhat Less	Substantially Less	

Question No. 24

Please rank the following *potential* computer problems in the order you believe would be the most disastrous for your organization (1=most problematic). Please do not assign tied ranks.

Complete or partial interruption of business activities.	☐	46-53
Destruction of accounting and control records.	☐	
Material inaccuracies in accounting and control records.	☐	
Manipulation of accounting and control records to cover or effect irregularities.	☐	
Exposure of sensitive corporate information.	☐	
Other (please specify)	☐	
		54-55

Other (please specify)	☐	
		56-57

Other (please specify)	☐	
		58-59

Question No. 25

If there are any special strengths or weaknesses of your company's internal control system that you feel should be included in its evaluation, please describe them briefly here. Add supplementary sheets if necessary.

Thank you for your participation. It is very much appreciated.

References

AICPA (1983) "Heinz Bill Easing FCPA Violation Penalties Gains SEC Support", *Journal of Accountancy* (April, 1983) p. 12.

AICPA (1979) *Report of the Special Advisory Committee on Internal Accounting Control* (New York: American Institute of Certified Public Accountants, 1979).

AICPA (1978) *Codification of Statements on Auditing Standards, Nos. 1 to 21* (New York: American Institute of Certified Public Accountants, 1978).

AICPA (1977) *Commission on Auditors' Responsibilities, Report on Tentative Conclusions* (New York: American Institute of of Certified Public Accountants, 1977).

Brown, Nander, (1983) "Minicomputers Control, Security and Audit", *The Internal Auditor* (February, 1983) pp. 39-42.

Catania, Salvatore C., Walter J. Dick and Martin E. Silverman (1980) *Contingency Planning: A Discussion of Strategies* (U.S.A.: Coopers and Lybrand, 1980).

CICA (1981) *Audit Committees* (Toronto: The Canadian Institute of Chartered Accountants, 1981).

CICA (1978) "Report of the Special Committee to Examinine the Role of the Auditor", (The Adams Report) *CA Magazine* (April, 1978) pp. 36-70.

CICA (1975) *Computer Audit Guidelines* (Toronto: The Canadian Institute of Chartered Accountants, 1975).

CICA (1970) *Computer Control Guidelines* (Toronto: The Canadian Institute of Chartered Accountants, 1970).

Canadian Institute of Chartered Accountants *CICA Handbook*, Sections 5200 - 5220.

Committee on Auditing Procedure (1972) "The Auditor's Study and Evaluation of Internal Control," *Statement on Auditing Procedure No. 54* (New York: American Institute of Certified Public Accountants, 1972).

Cooke, John E. and Brian R. Dobing (1984) *Management Control of Computer-Related Errors* (Hamilton: The Society of Management Accountants of Canada, 1984).

Coopers and Lybrand (1977) "EDP Security: A Perspective for Management", *Coopers and Lybrand Newsletter* (December, 1977).

Coopers and Lybrand (1983) *EDP Security: A Management Responsiblity* (Canada: Coopers and Lybrand, 1983).

Dearborn, D.C. and H.A. Simon (1958) "Selective Perception: A Note on the Departmental Identifications of Executives," *Sociometry* (1958) pp. 140-144.

Dewar, Douglas (1983) "Micros: A Challenge for Accountants," *Accountancy* (January, 1983) pp. 96-97.

Financial Executives Institute Canada (1981) *Integrity in Business* (Canada: Financial Executives Institute, 1981).

Fisher, Marguerite (1978) "Internal Controls: Guidelines for Management Action," *Journal of Accounting, Auditing and Finance* (Summer, 1978) pp. 349-360.

Fletcher, John C. (1981) "In Search of the Elusive Definition of 'Internal Control'," *The Internal Auditor* (June, 1981) pp. 39-45.

Fogler, Robert A. and Glen R. Sanderson (1983) "A Control Framework for Distributed Computer Systems," *The Internal Auditor* (October, 1983) pp. 71-78.

Foh, Noreen (1983) "The Auditor's Role in Pre-Implementation Reviews," *The CA Magazine* (May, 1983) pp. 75-77.

The Institute of Internal Auditors (1978) *Standards for the Professional Practice of Internal Auditing* (Altamonte Springs: Institute of Internal Auditors' Inc., 1978).

International Federation of Accountants (1981) "Study and Evaluation of the Accounting System and Related Internal Controls in Connection With an Audit," Auditing Guidelines in the IFAC *Handbook* (International Federation of Accountants, July, 1981) p. 9-41.

Jenkins, Brian, and Anthony Pinkney (1978) *The Audit Approach to Computers* (London: Institute of Chartered Accountants in England and Wales, 1978).

Kerlinger, Fred N. (1973) *Foundations of Behavioral Research* (Toronto: Holt, Rinehart and Winston, Inc., 1973).

Lee, T. A. (1971) "The Historical Development of Internal Control from the Earliest Times to the End of the Seventeenth Century," *Journal of Accounting Research* (Spring, 1971) pp. 150-157.

Macdonell, James J. (1979) "Value for Money: The Accountability Equation" a paper presented to the Institute of Public Administration of Canada (August 29, 1979).

Maher, Michael W. (1981) "The Impact of Regulation on Controls: Firms' Response to the Foreign Corrupt Practices Act," *The Accounting Review* (October, 1981) pp. 751-770.

Mastromano, Frank, editor (1982a) "Control and Security: Manual versus Computer Systems," in the Management Information Systems column of *Management Accounting* (August, 1982) pp. 10 and 66.

Mastromano, Frank, editor (1982b) "Improving Data Control", in the Management Information Systems Column of *Management Accounting* (October, 1982b) pp. 12 and 78.

Mautz, Robert K., Walter G. Kell, Michael W. Maher, Alan G. Merten, Raymond R. Reilly, Dennis G. Severance, and Bernard J. White (1980) *Internal Control in U.S. Corporations* (New York: Financial Executives Research Foundation, 1980).

Mautz, Robert K., Alan G. Merten and Dennis G. Severance (1983) *Senior Management Control of Computer-Based Information Systems* (Morristown: Financial Executives Research Foundation, 1983).

Mautz, Robert K. and James Winjum (1981) *Criteria for Management Control Systems* (New York: Financial Executives Research Foundation, 1981).

McQueary, Glenn M. II, and Michael P. Risdon (1979) "How We Comply with the Foreign Corrupt Practices Act," *Management Accounting* (November, 1979) pp. 39-43.

Page, John and Paul Hooper (1982) "Internal Control in Computer Systems," *Financial Executive* (June, 1982) pp. 14-20.

Perry, William (1983) *Auditing Information Systems: A Step-by-Step Approach* (Carol Stream: EDP Auditors Foundation, 1983).

Perry, William (1977) "The Internal Audit Mandate in EDP," *CA Magazine* (September, 1977) pp. 38-43.

Porter, W. Thomas and William E. Perry (1981) *EDP Controls and Auditing*, Third Edition (Boston: Kent Publishing Company, 1981).

Snedecor, George and Willian Cochran (1967) *Statistical Methods*, Sixth Edition (Ames: University of Iowa Press, 1967) pp. 258-377.

Society of Management Accountants of Canada (1984) *Management Accounting Guideline No. 3, Framework for Internal Control*, Exposure Draft (Hamilton: The Society of Management Accountants of Canada, August 1984).

U.S. Government Accounting Office (1972) *Standards for Audit of Governmental Organizations, Programs, Activities, and Functions* (Washington, D. C.: U.S. Government Printing Office, 1972).